UNDERSTANDING THE HEART SUTRA

Hiểu về Bát-nhã Tâm kinh

UNDERSTANDING the Heart Sutra

HIỂU VỀ BÁT NHÃ TÂM KINH

Drupa Rinpoche

CONTENTS

AUTHOR'S NOTE

The contents of this book are from the teaching transcripts of a Dharma class on Heart Sutra that I gave at Khacholing Center, Minneapolis, MN. The pictures are some of the slides that were used during class. Upon receiving suggestions and requests for the transcripts to be published into a book for those seeking foundational guidance into the profound topic of emptiness, I embarked upon this task.

Publication of this bi-lingual book has been made possible through the generous sponsorship of Madam Nga Thi Ngoc Nguyen, a sincere Dharma practitioner and energetic supporter of Dharma works, who also arranged for the book to be translated into Vietnamese by Ngakpa Kunga Lodro Thinh Nguyen. I also wish to acknowledge with appreciation the help of Yeo Puay Huei who encouraged me15 to do this book and helped with the editing of it.

Any mistakes made in this book are mine alone for which I extend my deepest apologies. Nonetheless, this book comes with my earnest prayers for it to be ableto offer at least one person some understanding of emptiness, offer some illumination on the path to enlightenment and offer some relief and comfort from the ocean of samsara.

Drupa Rinpoche

His Eminence Thích Quảng Tùng

Foreword by His Eminence Thich Quang Tung - Vice President of Vietnam Buddhist Sangha

The Heart Sutra (Prajñāpāramitā Hṛdaya) holds a place of extraordinary importance within both the Mahāyāna and Vajrayāna traditions of Buddhism. As a long-time practitioner devoted to the study and application of the essential teachings found in the Avataṃsaka, Śūraṅgama, Vimalakīrti, Lotus, Laṅkāvatāra, and Prajñāpāramitā sūtras, I am deeply moved and sincerely rejoice in this work by Venerable Drupa Rinpoche (Lobsang Yeshi). I also take this opportunity to commend the Vietnamese translator (Ngakpa Kunga Lodro Thinh Nguyen) and the Center for Vietnam Applied Buddhist Studies for their dedicated translation efforts, which have helped make this profound teaching more accessible to Vietnamese-speaking audiences.

In Tibetan Buddhism, sacred scriptures are traditionally preserved through woodblock printing. Although the Buddha taught extensively during his lifetime, none of his teachings were committed to writing while he was alive. His words were transmitted orally, remembered and recited by disciples of remarkable meditative concentration and mnemonic capacity. Only after the Buddha's Parinirvāṇa were his teachings compiled through great councils, where senior disciples chanted the sūtras in unison and transcribed them with fidelity and precision.

A well-known legend holds that after the Buddha's passing, celestial beings, asuras, and nāgas gathered to discuss who would safeguard the Dharma. Failing to reach consensus, the scriptures were said to have been dispersed in all directions. One account asserts that the Prajñāpāramitā scriptures were entrusted to the nāga realm and later retrieved by Nāgārjuna Bodhisattva. However, the nāgas did not release the entire corpus, retaining certain chapters to ensure Nāgārjuna's return. This is why some versions of the Prajñāpāramitā canon appear to be incomplete. Regardless of the geographical and cultural contexts in which these stories evolved, such historical narratives highlight the shared reverence among Buddhist traditions for the Buddha's teachings. They also underscore the invaluable contributions of translators in making these teachings available across linguistic and cultural boundaries.

Before offering commentary on the Heart Sutra, Drupa Rinpoche skillfully outlines the four principal schools of Buddhist philosophy and their respective views on anātman (non-self): the Vaibhāṣika, Sautrāntika, Cittamātra (Mind-Only), and Madhyamaka (Middle Way) schools - the latter further subdivided into Svātantrika and Prāsaṅgika. The first two schools do not assert the non-self of phenomena, while the latter two do, and it is upon this foundational insight that the path to complete enlightenment rests.

In particular, the Madhyamaka-Prāsaṅgika view - which upholds the inseparability of dependent origination and emptiness - is regarded as the most profound. It rejects the notion that phenomena possess any intrinsic existence, even as a basis for conceptual designation. All phenomena are seen as lacking inherent nature, existing only through dependence upon causes, conditions, and conceptual imputation. This perspective becomes especially crucial in approaching the Heart Sutra, a scripture that distills the essence of śūnyatā (emptiness) with unparalleled precision.

Despite their doctrinal differences, all four schools agree that the "self" does not exist independently from the five aggregates. What we call "self" arises in dependence on the aggregates and is merely a conventional label imposed by the mind. This foundational understanding is key to interpreting the Heart Sutra, which, although concise, penetrates directly to the heart of ultimate reality - a domain beyond the reach of conceptual elaboration.

For centuries, the Heart Sutra has served as a spiritual companion to monastics and lay practitioners alike. In both Tibetan and Vietnamese Mahāyāna traditions, it is recited daily by monastics and householders. Yet, due to its profound content - which transcends conventional language and conceptual frameworks - the Heart Sutra cannot be fully grasped through intellectual reasoning alone. Its realization depends upon direct insight into emptiness, an insight that has inspired countless commentaries by scholars, philosophers, and practitioners through the ages. These works, though vast in number and deeply profound, can never exhaust the meaning of the Heart Sutra, for the teachings of Mahāyāna Buddhism are boundless and immeasurable - accessible only through realization and lineage transmission.

Even so, Venerable Drupa Rinpoche, in his characteristic humility, remarks in this book:

"I cannot go as deep into this subject as one might hope. I don't have the wisdom or capacity to present it in great detail. So, unfortunately for you, you've ended up with me to help you understand this sutra somewhat. Nevertheless, I will try to go line by line through the sutra and provide some explanations. In Tibetan, this method is called tsig-'drel, which means explaining each word or phrase individually."

This approach is not only accessible but also faithful to the Tibetan exegetical tradition, and it gently reminds us of a central error: our deep-seated, mistaken perception of a real, independent self. We fabricate a sense of identity around a conceptual "I" and suffer immensely for it. Yet, as the Heart Sutra teaches, there is no truly existent "self" - only a name superimposed upon the aggregates of body and mind.

This, in essence, is the core message of the Heart Sutra - the distilled wisdom of the entire Prajñāpāramitā corpus. I am therefore honored to commend this work to venerable elders, monastics, Dharma teachers, scholars, and international readers who seek to deepen their understanding of the profound path of emptiness.

Vietnam, August 8, 2025

His Eminence Thích Quảng Tùng

Vice President, Central Executive Council, Vietnam Buddhist Sangha

Chairman, Central Committee for Buddhist Charity, Vietnam Buddhist Sangha

Head of the Vietnam Buddhist Sangha – Hải Phòng Province

Most Venerable Ottamathara

Foreword by Most Ven. Ottamanthara

The Buddha declared in the Aṅguttara Nikāya (Book of Eights, Chapter on the Great Ones):

"Just as the great ocean has but one taste-the taste of salt-so too, this Dhamma and Discipline has but one taste-the taste of liberation."

The primary audience for the Buddha's teachings has always been human beings living in this world, and though the historical development of Buddhism saw early signs of sectarian division even during the Buddha's lifetime, today we recognize three major Buddhist traditions: Theravāda, Mahāyāna, and Vajrayāna, along with countless schools and lineages derived from them.

Despite this diversity, the foundational principles of the Dhamma remain unchanged. Each tradition presents its own path of practice aimed at liberation from saṃsāra-helping sentient beings discern wholesome from unwholesome actions, guiding them to transform ignorance into wisdom, and to progress from ordinary beings to awakened ones. What truly governs rebirth within the three realms (the realm of desire, the realm of form, and the formless realm) is karma-our actions. Truth remains constant, regardless of whether or not a Buddha appears in the world. The Buddha merely revealed what was already there: the unchanging law of dependent origination and cessation.

The Buddha, having fulfilled innumerable pāramīs across countless lifetimes, attained Supreme Perfect Enlightenment (Sammāsambuddha), and was honored with the ten epithets, revered as the teacher of gods and humans. His realization was independent and self-arisen-without a teacher-thus his proclamation: "Above the heavens and below the heavens, I alone am the honored one." It is exceedingly rare for a Fully Enlightened Buddha to appear in this world, and when such a one arises, he reveals the Noble Path for the benefit of all beings.

For over twenty years, I have taught Vipassanā meditation and established more than 125 meditation centers under the name Thabarwa across Myanmar and in both the Eastern and Western hemispheres. In our teachings, we emphasize the importance of direct meditative practice. True Dhamma is only realized through experience-not through philosophical speculation or rigid adherence to conceptual views. Thus, I always instruct my students to ground themselves in conventional truth (sammuti-sacca), and to observe the natural law of cause, condition, and effect. For practitioners struggling with strong attachment, I teach them to cultivate unceasing and unconditional acts of goodness-"just do good," I say, "do it consistently, do it endlessly. This body and mind exist only to be used for that."

Human beings often find it easier to engage in unwholesome actions than to sustain wholesome conduct. Therefore, I urge my students to engage in virtuous deeds even more diligently, for the tendency toward unwholesome karma is pervasive in this age of moral laxity.

Venerable Drupa Rinpoche (Lobsang Yeshi), in this work, also points out a critical distinction: beings in the Kāmadhātu (Desire Realm), including humans, are driven by sensory pleasures. Beings in the Rūpadhātu (Form Realm) have renounced coarse sensual desires and seek refined meditative bliss. Ultimately, they progress toward equanimity and neutral feeling. Beings in the Arūpadhātu (Formless Realm) abandon material form altogether, abiding solely in increasingly subtle absorptions: the sphere of infinite space, infinite consciousness, nothingness, and neither perception nor non-perception.

Many non-Buddhist traditions in India regarded these meditative states as the final goal-liberation. However, in the Buddhist view, unless these absorptions are paired with wisdom-specifically, insight into emptiness, the conditioned and impermanent nature of all compounded phenomena-practitioners remain ensnared by ignorance and continue to revolve within saṃsāra.

The Buddha realized two core forms of clinging: self-clinging (attavāda) and clinging to phenomena (dhammavāda). These are the roots of craving and thus the root of suffering. This is why, at Thabarwa Meditation Centers, alongside Vipassanā practice, we emphasize 24-hour mindfulness in all postures, cultivating clear seeing of impermanence, dependent origination, and non-substantiality. This awareness leads to natural letting go.

Our mission has extended beyond contemplative practice. Amid Myanmar's political instability and civil strife, we have worked tirelessly to provide tangible social welfare: offering refuge and support to the elderly, terminally ill, the homeless, single mothers, orphans, the mentally ill, and those living with HIV/AIDS. We actively engage in environmental protection, waste recycling, and peace advocacy. These efforts reflect a deep resonance with the Mahāyāna ideal of bodhisattva conduct-embodied through the Four Immeasurables (loving-kindness, compassion, empathetic joy, and equanimity) and the Four Means of Embracing (generosity, kind speech, beneficial conduct, and empathetic participation).

The Heart Sutra is a revered text, long translated into English, and deeply rooted in the teachings of emptiness, non-clinging, non-abiding, and transcendent mindfulness. These principles are entirely in harmony with the essence of Vipassanā meditation, which cultivates direct realization of ultimate truth-paramattha-sacca, the Buddha-nature (Tathāgatagarbha), and the innate knowing.

In contemporary times, great Theravāda teachers such as Ajahn Chah in Thailand and Venerable Thích Viên Minh in Vietnam (of Bửu Long Monastery, Ho Chi Minh City), though rooted in the Theravāda tradition, have clearly demonstrated deep realization of emptiness and dependent origination.

This book by Venerable Drupa Rinpoche (Lobsang Yeshi) represents a vital contribution to the development of international Buddhism. It embodies the spirit of non-self, compassion, and the Middle Way. It supports the global aim of sustainable peace and spiritual awakening for humanity, as emphasized in the United Nations Day of Vesak 2025.

I wholeheartedly praise the altruistic spirit of Venerable Drupa Rinpoche and deeply appreciate the transmission of the Heart Sutra's teaching on emptiness, which offers a compass for both practitioners and humanity to cultivate compassion and work together for a more awakened and peaceful world.

United States, August 10, 2025

Most Venerable Ottamathara

Founder and Abbot of over 125 international Thabarwa Meditation Centers

Ph.D. in Philosophy, Mexico

Honorary Doctorate, India

International Affairs Committee, Center for Vietnam Applied Buddhist Studies

Associate Professor
Dr. Frank J.R. Guo (Guō Kē-Shuì)

Foreword by Dr. Frank J.R. Guo

The Heart Sutra encapsulates the very essence of the Prajñāpāramitā teachings. According to the Mahāyāna tradition, the Buddha taught an immeasurable variety of Dharma teachings - traditionally enumerated as 84,000 Dharma doors or collections of Dharma - which were delivered across three distinct turnings of the Dharma Wheel (Dharmacakrapravartana).

1. The First Turning centered on the teaching of the Four Noble Truths.
2. The Second Turning, to which the Heart Sutra belongs, introduced the profound doctrine of Prajñāpāramitā, or emptiness (śūnyatā).
3. The Third Turning offered clarification and further articulation of the teachings on emptiness.

After attaining unsurpassed awakening (anuttarā samyaksaṃbodhi), the Buddha initially remained silent, recognizing the profound depth of his realization as something beyond the comprehension of ordinary beings. It was only after the earnest request of Śakra (Indra), Lord of the Devas, that the Buddha delivered his first sermon at Deer Park,

Sarnath - the discourse on the Four Noble Truths.

In the Noble Eightfold Path, the practice of right view and right wisdom involves insight into emptiness - inseparable from the law of dependent origination. It was Nāgārjuna, the great Indian ācārya, who elevated the doctrine of śūnyatā to its highest expression through his treatise Mūlamadhyamakakārikā (Fundamental Verses on the Middle Way).

In this work, Venerable Drupa Rinpoche (Lobsang Yeshi) thoughtfully cites the renowned Tibetan master Je Tsongkhapa, who in The Three Principal Aspects of the Path wrote:

"Without the wisdom realizing the ultimate nature of reality, even if you cultivate renunciation and bodhicitta, you will be unable to cut through the root of saṃsāra."

In other words, no liberation from suffering is possible without insight into emptiness. For our Sangha at the Fuchih Dharma Foundation in Taiwan, Tsongkhapa's teachings - particularly his Great Treatise on the Stages of the Path (Lamrim Chenmo) - serve as a guiding framework for practice. It systematically lays out the progressive stages of the path:

1. Foundational Practices: relying on a qualified teacher, understanding the value of the human life and impermanence.

2. Common with the Lesser Vehicle: refuge and karma; cultivating ethical conduct and aiming for favorable rebirth.

3. Common with the Intermediate Vehicle: practicing the Four Noble Truths and Twelve Links of Dependent Origination, striving for liberation.

4. Unique to the Greater Vehicle: cultivating bodhicitta, practicing the Six Perfections and Four Means of Attraction to benefit all beings and ultimately attain Buddhahood.

Drupa Rinpoche also categorizes four types of Prajñāpāramitā:

1. Essential Prajñā (svabhāva-prajñā): the nature of emptiness itself.
2. Textual Prajñā: the scriptural teachings expounding emptiness.
3. Path Prajñā: the meditative insight into emptiness cultivated on the path.
4. Resultant Prajñā: the perfected wisdom of a fully awakened Buddha.

Textual Prajñā, in particular, is expressed through scriptures of varying length and depth:

- Extensive Version: 100,000 verses (Śatasāhasrikā).
- Intermediate Version: 25,000 verses (Pañcaviṃśatisāhasrikā).
- Abridged Version: 8,000 verses (Aṣṭasāhasrikā).
- Essential Version: The Heart Sutra, distilled like clarified butter from milk - the most concentrated expression of the Prajñāpāramitā corpus.

I deeply resonate with Rinpoche's exposition of the Prāsaṅgika Madhyamaka view. Regardless of whether a practitioner follows the Śrāvakayāna, Pratyekabuddhayāna, or Mahāyāna path, if one clings to notions of self or objective existence of phenomena, realization of emptiness becomes extremely difficult. The wisdom aspect of the path lies in the direct insight that all phenomena are merely conceptual projections, lacking independent or inherent nature. They exist only in dependence on conditions.

With such understanding, the practitioner can skillfully manifest body, speech, and mind within conventional reality, practicing bodhisattva conduct - bringing peace and benefit to sentient beings through the non-dual realization of "no-self and no-phenomena." In this way, one simultaneously liberates oneself and others.

I sincerely commend this work and wholeheartedly recommend it to international readers. May it contribute to the flourishing of Buddhist wisdom, and the collective efforts to build a civilized, compassionate, and sustainable global society - in alignment with the vision of the United Nations Day of Vesak 2025, held in Vietnam.

Taiwan, August 2025

Associate Professor Dr. Frank J.R. Guo (Guō Kē-Shuì)

Executive Director, Fuchih Culture & Education Foundation, Taiwan

President, Global Confucian Preservation Organization

Former Lecturer, National Kaohsiung University of Health Sciences

OVERVIEW

The Heart Sutra is a very well-known sutra. I believe most Buddhist traditions have it in their own language and their own version of it. Among Tibetans, the Heart Sutra is one of the most commonly recited daily prayers. It is recited before every teaching session, especially those led by His Holiness the Dalai Lama.

Despite its popularity and ubiquity, it remains deeply profound and difficult to understand. At its core is the teaching on emptiness. The Heart Sutra and anything related to the concept of emptiness, is often referred to as *"ma sam joe mi"*, which means "inconceivable", beyond ordinary words, beyond ordinary conception. Even those who have gained deep insight into emptiness find it challenging to explain. So, naturally, I struggle to explain this as well.

The Heart Sutra can be taught at many levels. Great teachers can spend days expounding its philosophical dimensions. In the *Lamrim Chenmo*, just the section on the "object of negation" spans 30 to 60 pages. Many scholars in the past have misunderstood the Buddha's teaching on emptiness. Because of this, texts like the *Lamrim Chenmo* emphasize the importance of a precise understanding of what is being negated when we say something is "empty."

I cannot go that deep into the subject. I don't have the insight or capacity to explain it in great detail. So, that's your misfortune -you've ended up with me to help you gain some understanding of this Sutra. Nonetheless, I will attempt to go through the text line by line and provide some explanation. In Tibetan, this approach is called *tsig-'drel*- explaining each word or phrase.

The Heart Sutra has long been translated into English and upon first reading, itmay appear deceptively simple. But unless one has some understanding of emptiness, it won't make much sense. Phrases like "no eye, no ear, no nose…" can seem confusing. However, once the concept of emptiness is understood, it all begins to make sense. That's our goal here - to try and understand what this profound text is actually pointing to.

What is the Heart Sutra?

It is known as the *Essence of the Perfection of Wisdom Sutra*. The Buddha gave countless teachings-traditionally summarized as 84,000 heaps of teachings-and these were given in stages, often classified as the *Three Turnings of the Wheel of Dharma.* The First Turning focused on the teachings of the 4 Noble Truths. The Second Turning dealt with the Perfection of Wisdom (emptiness) teachings. The Third Turning of the Wheel clarified the Buddha's teachings on emptiness. The

Heart Sutra relates to the teachings on emptiness given during the Second Turning of the Wheel of Dharma.

After attaining enlightenment, the Buddha initially remained silent. He felt that what he had realized was so radical, so revolutionary, that people simply wouldn't understand. It went against everything people believe about reality. Eventually, after being requested by the king of the gods, the Buddha began to teach. His first teaching was the *Four Noble Truths*, given at Sarnath.

We're all striving to be happy and avoid suffering. To achieve this, the Buddha said we must first recognize our suffering (the First Noble Truth). Most people only understand suffering as physical pain or gross discomfort, but the Buddha identified three types of suffering:

1. **The suffering of suffering** (obvious pain)

2. **The suffering of change** (what we mistake for pleasure is actually suffering because it changes)

3. **Pervasive conditioned suffering** (the deepest level, rooted in our conditioned existence)

To eliminate suffering, we must understand its causes (delusions/ afflictive emotions) - this is the Second Noble Truth. Once the causes are uprooted, suffering naturally ceases-this is the Third Noble Truth of cessation. To accomplish this cessation of suffering, we need to engage in the path (the methods to remove the delusions) - the Fourth Noble Truth. The ultimate path to sever the root of suffering is wisdom realizing emptiness. To elaborate on this path, the Buddha gave additional teachings, including the concept of *dependent origination,* which is the idea that everything (happiness and suffering) arises due to causes and conditions, with the principal cause being ignorance - ignorant about the empty nature of things.

In *Nagarjuna's Fundamental Wisdom*, he states:

"Obscured by ignorance, for the sake of rebirth, we create three types of actions,which construct existence and propel us through the cycle of samsara (cyclic existence)."

These are the actions/karmas that lead us to the three realms: Desire Realm (whichincludes the human realm and lower realms), the Form Realm and FormlessRealms. Even the higher level meditative states in the Formless Realms if not motivated by the aspiration for liberation from cyclic existence, still bind us to samsara. Lama Tsongkhapa, in *The Three Principal Aspects of the Path*, writes:

"Without the wisdom realizing ultimate reality, even if you generate renunciation and bodhicitta, you cannot cut the root of cyclic existence."In other words, without insight into emptiness, there is no way to eradicate suffering at its root. The Buddha (born as Prince Siddhartha) himself went throughan entire process to realize this. While living in the palace, Prince Siddhartha engaged in meditation and attained a certain degree of meditative concentration. Dissatisfied with that level of realization, he renounced royal life to become a monk. He then sought out renowned Hindu teachers of that time and continued meditating based on the instructions he received from them.

Upon attaining the highest form of meditative absorption- known as the absorption of the Peak of Samsara- Prince Siddhartha approached his teacher to ask what lay beyond. He was told that this peak was Nirvana and that there was nothing more to be taught. Siddhartha, however, was not convinced that the state he had reached was true emancipation and thus continued his search. To him, these various levels of concentration did not address the root of suffering. They merely reduced the objects of attachment but did not eliminate attachment at its root. While beings in the Desire Realm (which includes the human realm) chase after sensual pleasures, beings in Form Realm transcend sensual desire and instead seek pleasure derived from concentration, ultimately seeking a state of neutral feeling. Beings in the Formless Realms turn their focus from physical forms to the mind alone, subsequently progressing to state of concentration that focuses on nothing at all and eventually to the subtlest state of neither perception nor non- perception. Many non-Buddhist schools in India believe this as the final destination - Emancipation. However, the Buddhist perspective is that as long as these absorptions are not complimented by the wisdom realising emptiness, one would continue to be influenced by ignorance, remain in samsara and thereby subject to suffering.

Eventually, Prince Siddhartha realized that the two types of grasping-grasping ata falsely conceived, truly existing self, and grasping at phenomena-are the root causes of attachment, and thus the source of suffering.

In social situations such as family arguments, if we analyze deeply, we find the rootof the conflict is the strong sense of "I". We defend this "I," develop attachment tothose who support it, and react angrily toward those who threaten it. This false, solid "I" is the core of our problems. The teachings on emptiness examines thetrue nature of this seemingly absolute "I". This is why understanding emptiness- ultimately realizing that this "I" does not exist inherently-is so critical. It can truly be a panacea for our problems.

A great scholar once shared a story: A father with three sons divided his assets while he was still healthy. The two elder sons left the home, and one stayed back. This youngest son was entrusted with the care of the father. The other sons were indifferent and didn't help. A friend of the father saw this and devised a plan. He brought a large, heavy box, and told the father, "Here's the thing you asked me to return to you when you're in trouble." The box was locked, and the key hung fromthe father's neck.

The youngest son, assuming the box contained treasure, suddenly became very kind, attentive, and loving. The other sons noticed the change and learned of the box. They, too, began showing care for the father, hoping for a share. Eventually, the father passed away. They opened the box-and found only stones. They based all their actions on a false assumption.

This story reflects our relationship with the false sense of "I." We've built up an elaborate idea of a solid, concrete self. But in actuality, there is no inherently existing "I." There is merely a concept of "I" labelled on our aggregates (body and mind). We suffer and toil for this illusion-like "I". This is the essence of the Heart Sutra which is part of the Second Turning of the Wheel of Dharma. The Heart Sutra distils the *essence of the Perfection of Wisdom* (*Prajnaparamita*) teachings on emptiness.

There are four types of "Perfection of Wisdom":

1. **Natural Perfection of Wisdom** - which is emptiness itself.

2. **Textual Perfection of Wisdom** - the scriptures explaining emptiness.

3. **Path Perfection of Wisdom** - the wisdom that realizes emptiness on thepath.

4. **Resultant Perfection of Wisdom** - the perfected wisdom of a fullyenlightened Buddha.

The textual category (scriptures) has several levels:

- **Extensive version** (Bhum) - 100,000 verses
- **Middle version** - (Nyi Tri) - 25,000 verses
- **Short version** (Gye Tongpa) - 8,000 verses
- **Essence version** - the Heart Sutra

During special days or rituals, monks read these texts, especially the 8000 verse "Gye Tongpa". It takes several days to recite the extensive versions, while the Heart Sutra is condensed like butter churned from milk, the purest essence of the teachings.

When I was young, my father used to churn butter by hand. First, he would make milk curd, then churn it in a wooden cylinder that has a propeller. He would wear an apron-not really an apron, but some sort of cloth-and start churning by repeatedly pushing and pulling the wooden propeller up and down the barrel. There was a rhythm to the way he churned it. He would engage in a count, where after every few hundred churns, he'd pour in a bit of warm water. Somehow, he would always know when the butter was ready. That moment always amazed me.

Why do I bring this up? Because the *Heart Sutra* is like the essence - like thebutter - from all the teachings of the Buddha. Just as butter is the result of churning milk and cream, the *Heart Sutra* is the distilled essence of the vast *Perfection of Wisdom* teachings. That's what we're going to try to understand here.

In Tibet, scriptures/sutras are traditionally printed from woodblocks. Each word is carved onto woodblocks. You can see photos where two men are printing texts - first, they carefully cut the paper to size, ink the woodblock, press the paper onto it, and then swipe to transfer the ink. It's a tedious process, but that's how the texts were created.

As regards how these sutras were preserved: the Buddha gave teachings in many places, but during his lifetime, nothing was written down. It was all passed on orally. After the Buddha's passing, great gatherings were held where his disciples who had memorized his teachings, recited them and these were notated. These were practitioners with advanced meditative powers and extraordinary memories, allowing them to remember teachings with great clarity and precision.

There's even a story that, after the Buddha passed away, beings gathered- humans, devas, asuras, nagas-and debated who should become the custodians of these sacred teachings. Unable to agree, the texts were said to have been dispersed in all directions. One tradition holds that the *Perfection of Wisdom* sutras were safeguarded in the realm of the Nagas (serpent-like beings), and that later, Nagarjuna visited the land of the Nagas and retrieved these texts. Interestingly, it's said the Nagas didn't return all the chapters - keeping some as insurance to encourage Nagarjuna's return. That's why, in some versions of the *Perfection of Wisdom Sutras*, certain chapters are missing.

Understanding the *Heart Sutra*: Philosophical Context

Before diving into the *Heart Sutra*, we need a basic understanding of the four major Buddhist philosophical schools and their views on no self or selflessness.

Views on Selflessness: Four Schools

Vaibhashika school – Selflessness of the Person
Suatrantika school – Selflessness of the Person
Cittamatra school (Mind-only school) – Selflessness of the Person & Selflessness of phenomena
Madhyamika school (Middle Way school) - Selflessness of the Person & Selflessness of phenomena
  Svatantrika school – Ultimate intrinsic existence
  Prasangika school - Ultimate intrinsic existence

Buddhist vs. Non-Buddhist Views on Self

Non-Buddhist traditions often assert that "self" is permanent, unitary, and independent, that means a self that exists apart from the body and mind (the aggregates). In contrast, Buddhists assert there is no self that exists independently of the aggregates. The self arises dependently. In other words, the self arises based on the aggregates.

There are four Buddhist philosophical schools, the first two, namely, **Vaibhashika** and **Sautrantika**- emphasize the selflessness of the person. They believe that realizing this is enough to attain **nirvana** or liberation. They do not discuss the selflessness of phenomena.

The next two schools - **Cittamatra** (Mind - Only) and **Madhyamika**-assert the selflessess of the person and the selflessness of phenomena. These schools aim beyond liberation; their goal is full **enlightenment** (Buddhahood). They address two levels of obscurations to attaining full enlightenment:

1. **Obscurations to liberation** (emotional afflictions),

2. **Obscurations to omniscience** (cognitive distortions).

To remove the second set of obscurations, one must realize not only the selflessness of the person but also the **selflessness of phenomena**.

Selflessness and Dependent Origination

Within these four schools, there are nuanced differences in how they understand selflessness. For instance, the **Prasangika Madhyamika** school (often termed as the highest philosophical school) asserts that nothing exists from its own side. In contrast, the other three schools believe there must be *some* inherently existing substance as a base. These three schools offer an analogy: To be called a doctor, a person must have studied medicine and gained qualifications. Only then can the label "doctor" be validly applied. For them, it's not enough to just label someone; there must be a basis that exists from its own side.

This is where the **Prasangika** view is unique - it claims that even that basis doesn't exist inherently. Everything, including the basis of designation, is empty of inherent existence. What we call "doctor" or "person" is merely labelled by mind, based on a collection of parts and functions - there is no intrinsic nature behind these labels. This becomes especially important when understanding the *Heart Sutra.* The text uses phrases like: "No eye, no ear, no nose... no form, no sound, no smell…"

To someone unfamiliar with emptiness, the above words appear nonsensical. But with insight into **emptiness** and **dependent origination** (that things come about in reliance upon factors such as causes, conditions, component parts and mental labels), it begins to make profound sense. The text isn't denying the conventional existence of these things; rather, it's negating their inherent or independent existence. In the lower Buddhist schools, they try to identify where the self is. Some of them point to the six consciousnesses and say, "That is the self." But in the *Mind-Only* (Cittamātra) school, they oppose that view by arguing that the six consciousnesses can't be the self and instead, point to particular consciousness which they call a storehouse consciousness, a repository of all karmic imprints, as the self. These perspectives arise from their belief that there must be some substance that exists from its own side. If you hold that view, then you must be able to identify a substantial, independently existing entity as the self or the object.

Other views might look at a thing like a mobile phone and say it's the aggregation of its parts that constitutes the phone. When applied to the self, they may point to consciousness. But the *Prāsaṅgika Madhyamika* view is different. They follow the Buddha's statement: **"There is no real substance."** Here, they assert **the selflessness of phenomena**.

In the *Prāsaṅgika* school, whether you are a Hinayana practitioner (a Hearer or Solitary Realizer) or on the Mahayana path, you cannot achieve the Liberation without realizing **emptiness of inherent existence**. The wisdom aspect of the path is the realization of emptiness. From the *Prāsaṅgika* point of view, the understanding of selflessness presented by the other schools is too coarse. It doesn't cut deep enough to uproot ignorance. So, they assert that things **do not exist from their own side** - they are merely mental projections

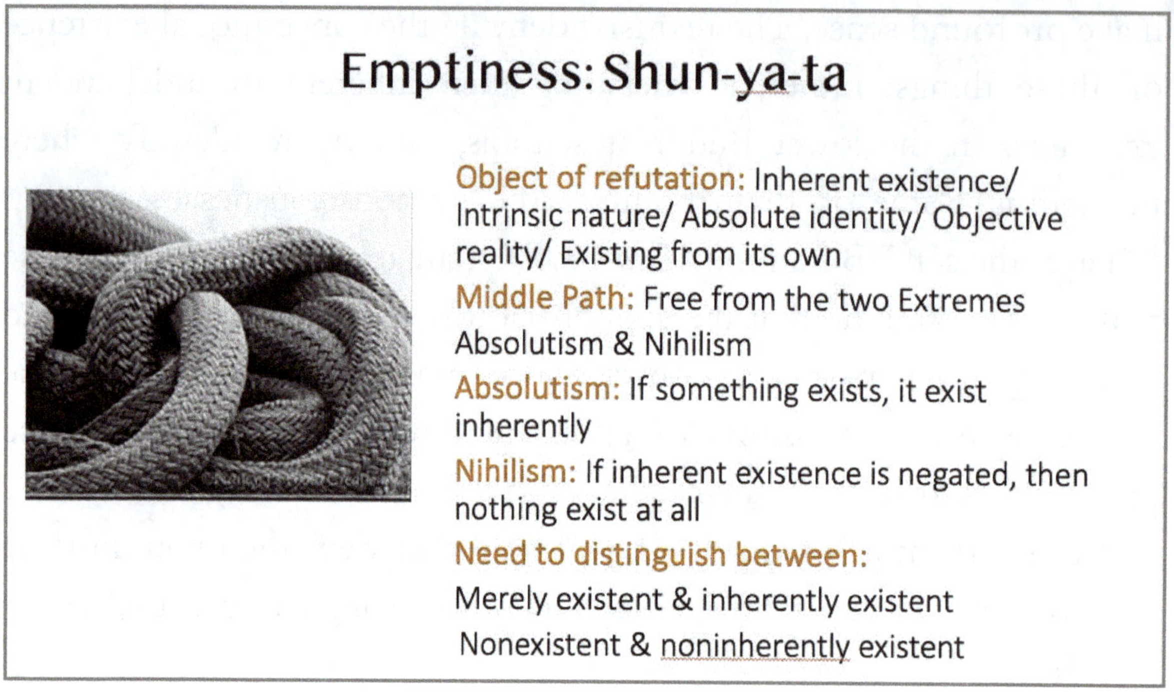

onto a base.

Let's look at the classic example given as an analogy: imagine you see a coiled rope in the dark. At first glance, it appears to be a snake. You feel fear - your heart races. But upon closer inspection, you realize it's just a rope. That fear, though based on a mistaken perception, was very real. The dream-like illusion of a snake caused a genuine emotional reaction. Similarly, in a dream, we might be terrified of a monster. That fear, the sweating, the heartbeat - all are real reactions to an unreal situation. The mind projects appearances. If things existed truly from their own side, that illusion wouldn't be possible. The *Prāsaṅgika* view is that things are like illusions, like dreams. What we see is a **mere projection** - not a reflection of inherent existence.

Projection and Perception

Imagine a movie projector. The screen itself is blank, like a tabula rasa. When the film rolls, images appear-vivid and engaging. But they are just projections. Likewise, the mind projects appearances onto people, things and situations, and we grasp at them as real. That's why the *Prāsaṅgika Madhyamaka* school hold that things exist merely by conceptual designation onto a base.

Real-Life Application

Someone once shared her experience at work. Her boss, who disliked her, scolded her harshly. In that moment, this person had an insight: "The unpleasantness of this scolding, of what I am hearing and seeing is just my mental projection. The boss is like a blank screen and my past negative karmic imprints are making me project negatively onto that screen (the boss)". Thinking this way allowed her anger to immediately subside, thereby ending her upset and suffering. It was replaced by a new understanding and a wish to help ease the situation. It enabled her to intuitively respond, "Is there anything I can help with?" The boss was stunned. Emotional transformation comes from understanding the nature of mental projections.

When we hear unpleasant things, we tend to get angry and react negatively. For instance, when a boss criticizes one's work as a "bad job," we often get stuck on the word "bad." However, by applying the understanding of emptiness and examining the phrase "bad job," we see that although it appears to exist solidly from its own side, there is *nothing inherently* bad about it. It is merely a label ascribed to an aspect of the work based on someone's perspective (the boss) and surrounding factors. There is nothing objectively or independently bad outside of the boss's perception and those factors. If the work were inherently bad, then everyone would see it that way no matter what. Yet, a colleague or a different boss or different factors might cause the same work to be viewed as excellent.

Another example illustrating the lack of inherent good or bad is weight gain. I learned that in Western culture, weight gain often carries a negative connotation and pointing it out is considered rude. In Tibetan culture, however, saying someone has gained weight is seen as a compliment. It is common for elderly Tibetans to comment on a person's weight and to express genuine concern if someone has lost weight. Similarly, they rejoice when someone appears to have gained weight. That's' why in Tibetan communities, people tend to react positively to such comments - feeling happy if they are told that they've gotten heavier and would be concerned if someone says they have become thinner. This is the opposite to how many people raised in Western culture would react. To Tibetan elders, gaining weight is good and losing weight is bad; in contrast, for many in the West, gaining weight is bad and losing weight is good.

The point is this: if good and bad existed inherently, everyone-regardless of cultural background - would perceive them the same way. Yet we find this not to be the case. Opposing conclusions to the same set of circumstances can arise. Therefore, applying the understanding of emptiness in our daily lives can protect us from unnecessary suffering.

From this we can see that even if we haven't fully realized emptiness, just **reflecting on it** can be incredibly beneficial. In the above case of the scolding boss, thinking about mental projections may not change the external situation but can halt one's suffering.

The Buddha said that even hearing about emptiness, or even **doubting** it, is highly meritorious. Imagine how beneficial deep study and reflection on it would be. The benefits of encountering the emptiness teachings - let alone reflecting and meditating on it - are vast. Even if one hears the teachings with a negative mind, benefits can still be derived from listening. There is an account of bodhisattva Manjushri giving teachings on emptiness to an assembly of persons, where a group of listeners didn't understand the meaning of the teaching. Feeling disgruntled, this group left the audience, complaining that Manjushri's talk on emptiness was incomprehensible and nonsensical. This criticism resulted in this group being born in the hell realms. Seeing this, Venerable Shariputra asked Manjushri why he taught emptiness to this group of persons who were now born in the hell realms. Manjushri answered that this group was already karmically destined for the lower realms but by virtue of them receiving the emptiness teachings, the duration of their being in the hell realms would be shortened.

Another example: During a turbulent flight, my friend who was a passenger became afraid. Underlying this panic was due to him grasping at a solid "I" which in turn instilled fear and worry over what would happen to this "I". But he reflected on emptiness and searched for the so-called solidity of the "I". Not finding this solid, truly existing I, the fear subsided. That's the practical application of these teachings. Through contemplation, if one is able to deconstruct this seemingly solid "I", the fear and worry that ensues would automatically subside.

As we study the Heart Sutra, we study not to merely accumulate knowledge. We must reflect on its lessons and apply them in daily life. Ask yourself:

- *How can I use this teaching?*

- *How does this help me understand my life experiences?*

When applied, the teachings become deeply personal and transformative.

Clarifying Emptiness

It's important to clarify what we are negating when we talk about emptiness. **We are not saying that things don't exist.** The Buddha never said that. When we say that things lack *inherent existence*, we mean they **do not exist independently** from their own side. Instead, things arise dependently in reliance on causes, conditions, component parts and conceptual designation.

This term - *inherent existence* - is used by all Buddhist schools, but each school defines it differently. That's why confusion arises. In English, we say things lack "intrinsic nature" or "inherent existence," but the *Prāsaṅgika* school takes this to its most subtle level. They assert that if things existed inherently, then they would not arise from causes and conditions. Things would not change or disintegrate. They would remain forever unchanging and static. But we can observe that everything **arises due to causes and conditions.** *There is that dependency and because of that, everything is empty of inherent existence.* Or put in another way, "All external and internal things are empty of inherent existence because they are dependently arisen". This prevents one from falling into either of the two extremes: absolutism or nihilism. Many tend to fall into one of these extremes. When told that things exist, they assume this means things exist inherently - this is the extreme of absolutism. On the other hand, when it's said that things do not exist inherently, they misunderstand this as meaning things do not exist at all - thus falling into the extreme of nihilism. When one can establish that things do exist (dependently), but not inherently, their view is said to follow the Middle Path - free from both extremes.

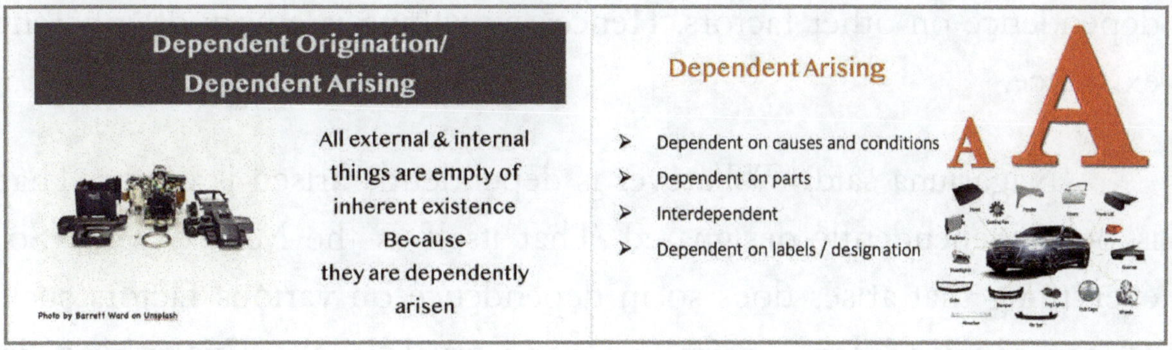

There are various types of dependent arising. The common one is that of dependence on causes and conditions. For example, plants depend on many causes such as seeds and conditions such as water, nutrients etc. All causes and effects fall into this category. Another type of dependent arising is dependent on parts. For instance, a car is dependent on its parts. Without the parts like wheels, engine etc, there is no car. Third type of dependent arising is called interdependence. This is where the existence of one thing is dependent or relative to another's existence. For instance, short and tall exist due to their relation to each other. When we say something is short, we are comparing it to something else. Same goes for big and small.

Finally, there is another type of dependent arising known as dependent on labels or conceptual thoughts. For example, the alphabet "A" exists because we are taught to call it that when we see a specific formation of lines. If we show the letter "A" to someone who does not know the alphabet, that person won't see the letter "A" but will only see 3 lines put together. This illustrates the role of mental imputation or labelling of things we observe. In the absence of mental imputation, the letter A will not exist. Its existence is dependent on a base (the 3 lines) and the mental imputation of "alphabet A". The above are the various types of dependent arising and all go toward supporting the view that things do not have inherent nature but arise in reliance or dependence on other factors. Hence, everything is empty of inherent existence.

Nāgārjuna said: "Whatever is dependently arisen is empty. That is being dependently designated. That itself is the Middle Way." So, everything that arises does so in dependence on various factors such as causes, conditions, parts, or conceptual labels. E**verything is empty of intrinsic, inherent existing**. And because of emptiness, **everything is possible**. Understanding dependent origination leads to the understanding of the Four Noble Truths of suffering, its origin, cessation, and the path.

Final thoughts

Some schools argue that if things don't inherently exist, then there's no difference between good and bad, virtue and non-virtue. But this is a misunderstanding. **Merely existing** is different from **inherently existing.** When we say things do not inherently exist, we are not saying they don't exist at all. Things do exist- *conventionally*. They function, they bring about happiness or suffering - but they are **empty of independent** existence. So, understanding this is crucial. If things truly existed from their own side, they would be fixed; they wouldn't change, age, or decay. They would not need causes or conditions to arise. But we see that things arise, change, and cease - all due to causes and conditions. Therefore, the *Prāsaṅgika* conclusion is: Everything exists dependently. Therefore, everything is empty. And because everything is empty, everything can arise.

INTRODUCTION

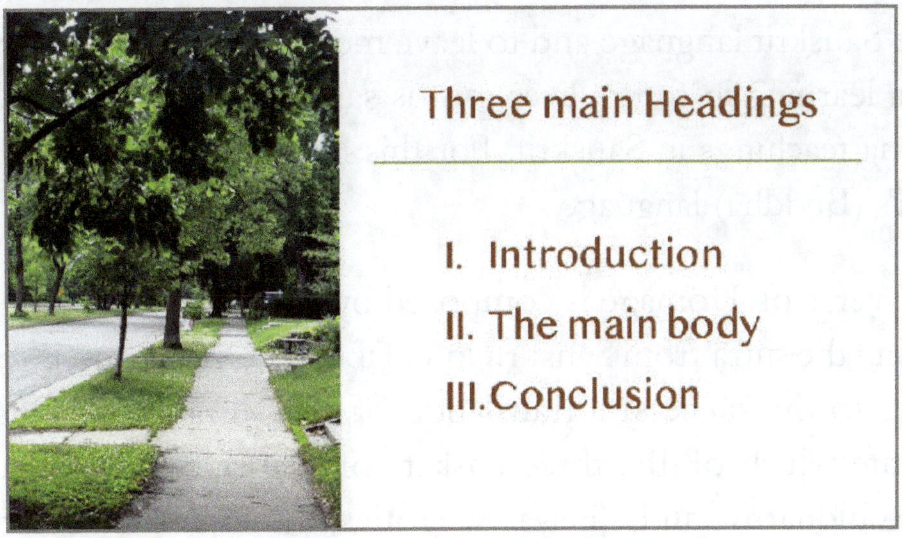

Heart Sutra is explained under three main headings: Introduction, the main body and the conclusion. Under Introduction, there are three sub-headings: The title of the sutra, homage and the context.

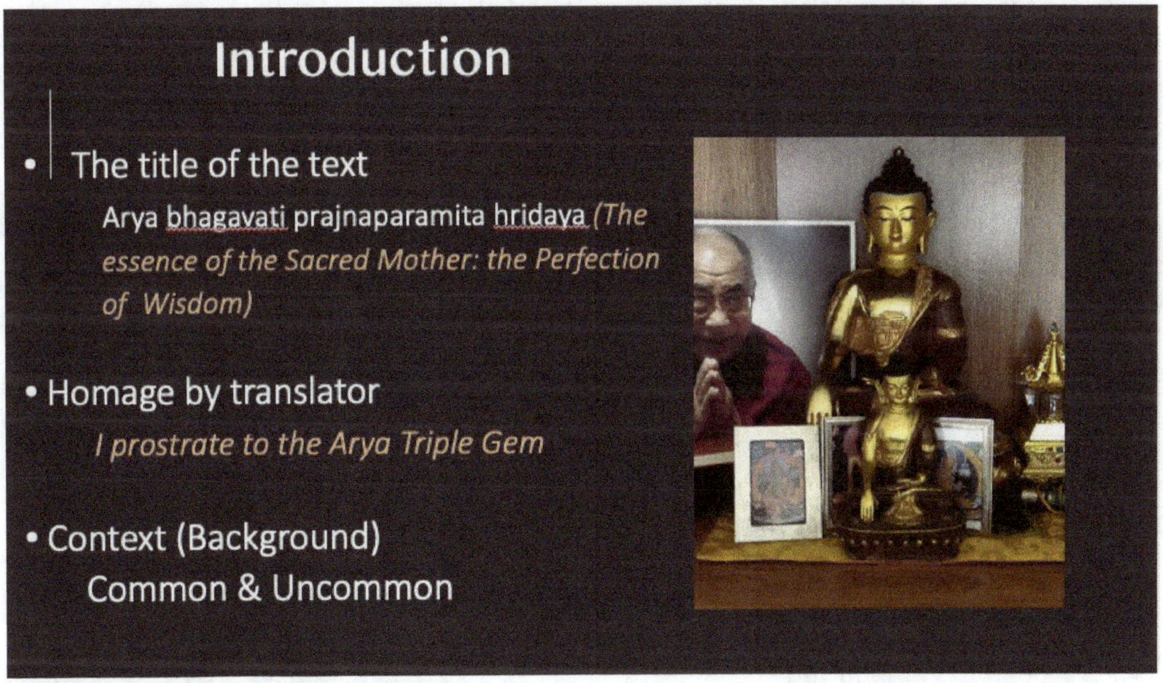

All Sutras translated into Tibetan have their titles in Sanskrit. One reason is to show the authenticity of the sutra. Since Buddhism started in India, India is considered a pure source of dharma. In order to show that this is an authentic teaching from India, the title of the sutra is purposely left in Sanskrit. Another reason is to help one gain familiarity with the Sanskrit language and to leave mental imprints to enable easier Dharma learning in future lives as it is said that all Buddhas will teach Mahayana teachings in Sanskrit. For this reason, Sanskrit is referred to as Deva's (Buddha) language.

A verse of Homage is composed by the translator at the time of translating the sutra from Sanskrit into Tibetan. One reason is to remove obstacles to the successful translation of the sutra. Another reason is to indicate which of the three baskets of the Buddha's teachings, i.e. Sutra, Abhidharma and Vinaya categories, the Sutra belongs to. From the homage, a reader can determine the main topic of the sutra. If the homage is made to the Omniscient Mind, the main content of the sutra is Vinaya (ethics). Homage to Manjushri indicates the main content of the sutra to be on wisdom. The sutras containing topics relating to concentration bear the homage to Buddhas and Bodhisattvas. So, the homage stanza has this purpose.

Context is about laying the background. There are two types of contexts: Common and uncommon context.

Common Context:

The perfect conditions:

The perfect time: Once
The perfect teacher: Shakyamuni Buddha
The perfect congregation of listeners: community of monks & Bodhisattvas
The perfect location: Vulture Peak, Rajgir

"Thus have I once heard: The Blessed....and great community of bodhisattvas,..."

Where the text begins with "*Thus have I once heard: The Bhagvan was staying in Rajdriha at Vulture Peak along with a great community of monks, and a great community of bodhisattvas*", it is called the common context because all sutras begins with this kind of background that provides information about the location where the teaching was given, the teacher, the time and the audience. In the case of the Heart Sutra, four perfect conditions are listed. Firstly, the perfect time: The sutra says, "*Thus have I once heard..*". This suggests the rarity of the teaching. Ananda who compiled this sutra is saying that although Buddha gave many teachings, the Heart Sutra was taught only once. So, this shows how precious and rare this teaching is. Another way to read this line is that Ananda heard it only once but was able to memorize it completely, thus suggesting the power of memory that Ananda possessed.

"*... the Bhagavan was staying in Rajgriha at Vulture's Peak along with a great community of monks and a great community of bodhisattvas*" . The Bhagavan refers to the second condition of the perfect teacher. Bhagavan literally means "the one who has destroyed all negativities and perfected all the qualities". In this case, Bhagavan refers to Shakyamuni Buddha. *Vulture's Peak* refers to the location or the place where this teaching was given. The hill on which Buddha gave this teaching is called Vulture's Peak because of its shape resembling a vulture. There are different versions of the origin of its name, but all involve a resemblance of the peak's shape to that of a vulture or its head or a gathering of a flock of vultures. *Great community of monks and a great community of bodhisattvas* refers to the perfect congregation. This tells us who were present during the teaching. As the sutra reads, there was a huge gathering consisting of many monks and many bodhisattvas, as well as beings from other realms.

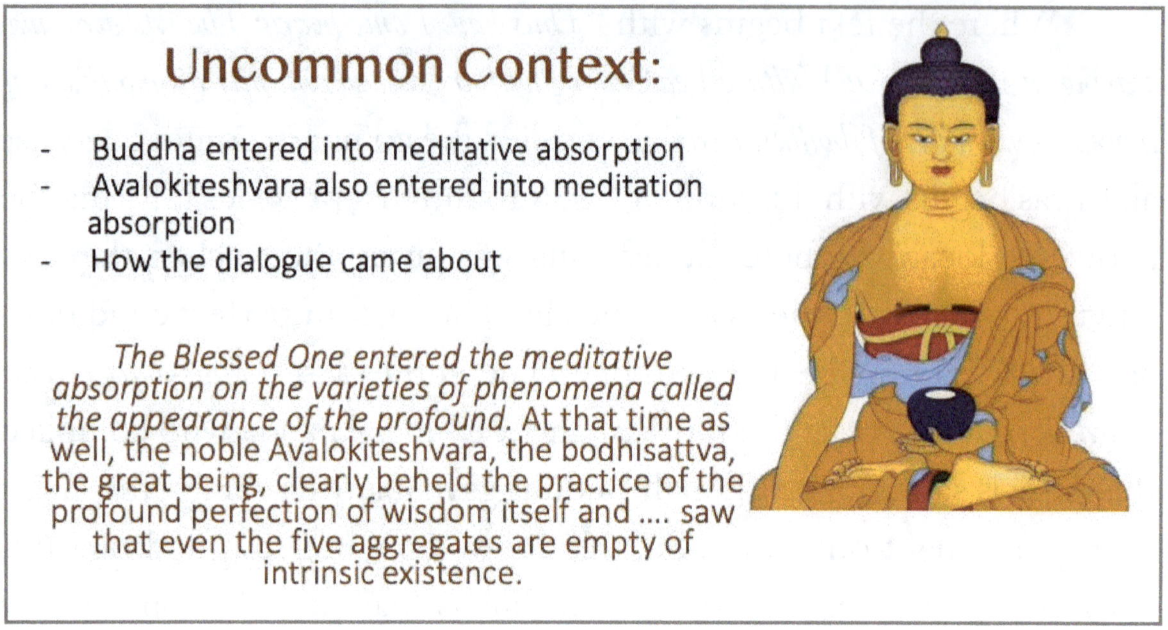

To inform the readers of the uncommon context, the Sutra reads; "*The Bhagavan entered the meditative absorption on the varieties of phenomena called the appearance of the profound. At that time as well, the noble Avalokiteshvara, the bodhisattva, the great being, clearly beheld the practice of the profound perfection of wisdom itself and saw that even the five aggregates are empty of intrinsic existence*". This is called uncommon context because this is unique to this teaching only. The uncommon context informs us two things:

(1) Buddha entered into meditative absorption: Technically, Buddha is always in meditative absorption. There is no period or time where Buddha is not in a meditative absorption. This is one of the many qualities of Buddha. Buddha can see the two truths of conventional truth and ultimate truth simultaneously. However, during Buddha's time in India, the practice was that after lunch, the Buddha would sometimes be in meditation and at other times, the Buddha would teach or give opportunity for the followers to ask questions. At the time of this Sutra teaching, Buddha chose to remain in meditation. There are numerous types of

concentrations that Buddha has achieved. During this time, the Buddha entered into meditation on the Profound Appearance or otherwise known as emptiness. Emptiness is commonly referred to as profound because it is ineffable - too profound to be easily explained or described in words.

(2) Avalokiteshvara also entered into meditation: At that time, Avalokiteshvara also entered into the meditation on emptiness and saw that five aggregates are empty of intrinsic existence. So, what are the five aggregates?

Five Aggregates

Aggregate of form	4 elements, 5 sense organs & sense objects
Aggregate of feeling	Pleasant, unpleasant & neutral
Aggregate of perception	Ability to discern, recognize and categorize
Aggregate of mental formation	Wholesome or unwholesome mental factors
Aggregate of consciousness	Six consciousness

The five aggregates are one way of classifying all the composite phenomena. Each aggregate has its unique function. Let's say, I saw a latest iPhone and I want to buy one. In this scenario, we can see the work of all the five aggregates. First my eye sense organ (eye faculty) has to come in contact with the iPhone (visible form). These two fall under the **aggregate of form**. The iPhone coming in contact with my eye faculty is not enough. It cannot make any sense of it. I need my eye consciousness to make sense of the object and hence the role of eye consciousness which falls under **the aggregate of consciousness**. There are five other consciousness. This is similar to how science explains that we need an object, retina and the brain to work together to generate a vision. As my eye consciousness makes me see the phone, at the same time, there develops other mental factors that enables me to discern/identify the object as an iPhone, as well as give rise to certain feeling (pleasant, unpleasant or neutral) towards that phone. That discerning mind and the feeling are **the aggregate of discrimination and aggregate of feeling** respectively. As a result of whatever feelings I develop upon seeing and recognizing the object, I also develop other mental attitudes such as liking, aversion or indifference. This mental state is known as **the aggregate of mental formation.** This is how our five aggregates function within us. Understanding the emptiness of the five aggregates i.e. how they arise in dependence of various factors and are not inherently existing, are crucial in developing the perfection of wisdom.

The text reads: *"Thereupon, through the Buddha's inspiration, the venerable Shariputra spoke to Avalokitesvara, the bodhisattva, the great being, and said, How should any noble son or noble daughter who wishes to engage in the practice of the profound perfection of wisdom train?"*. The first part informs the reader how the dialogue between Shariputra and Avalokiteshvara came about. In order to understand this, we need to look at the types of Buddha's teachings or sutras (Kaa). Buddha's teaching is defined as words or speech by Buddha. However, when we say speech by Buddha, it does not necessarily mean that the Buddha himself has spoken those words. Hence there are three types of Buddha's words.

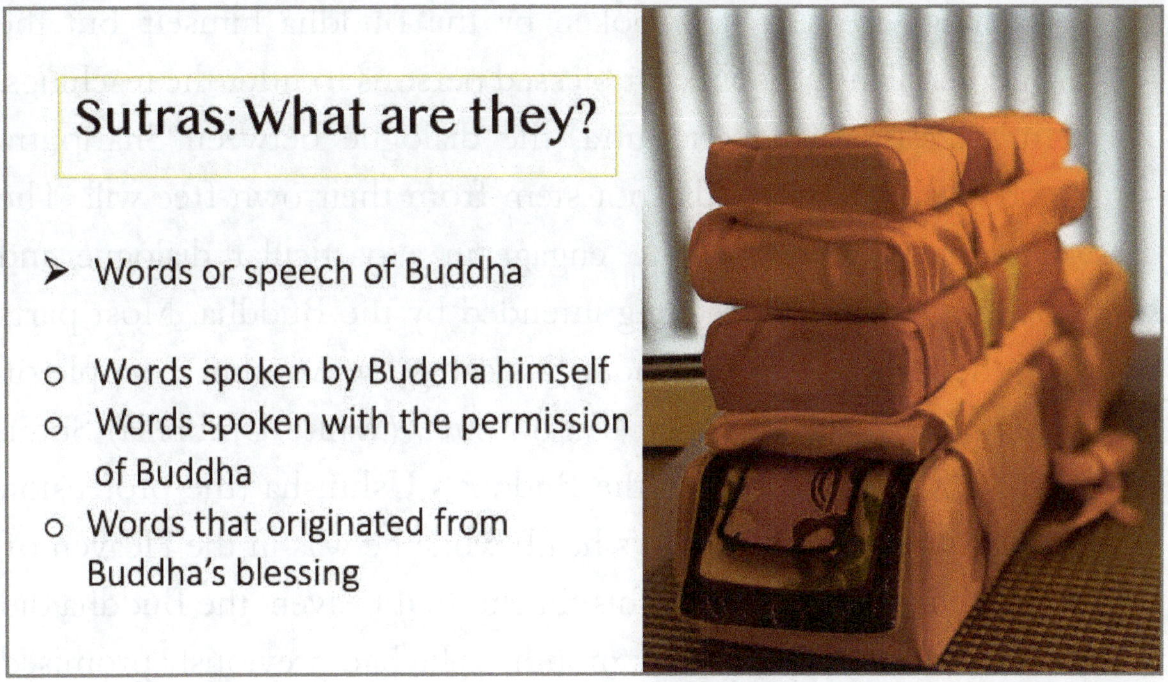

1. **Words spoken by the Buddha himself:** These are words of teachings spoken by the Buddha himself. The words were uttered by Buddha himself. An example of this type of Buddha's word appears toward the end of the Heart Sutra when Buddha commends Avalokiteshvara for an excellent presentation of the perfection of wisdom which reads *"Excellent! Excellent! O Noble child, it is just so; it should be just so. One must practice the profound perfection of wisdom just as you have revealed, For then even the tathagatas will rejoice."*

2. **Words spoken with the permission of the Buddha:** These are not spoken directly by the Buddha himself but instructed by the Buddha to do so. These are included by the compilers. For instance, the context of the Heart Sutra (Thus have I once heard…) which lays the background of theteaching falls under this category.

3. **The words that originated from Buddha's blessing:** These

teachings are also not spoken by the Buddha himself but the Buddha silently inspired or blessed persons to utter the teachings. In the case of Heart Sutra, the dialogue between Shariputra and Avalokiteshvara did not stem from their own free will. The Buddha inspired them to engage in a particular dialogue and brought forth the teaching intended by the Buddha. Most parts of the Heart Sutra fall under this category. Another example of this type of sutra is the *Arya Sitapatra* (White Umbrella) Sutra, which was spoken from the Buddha's Ushnisha (the protrusion at the top of the Buddha's head) while he was in the Heaven of the Thirty-Three. During his time in that heaven, the Buddha did not teach directly from his mouth, as he had previously promised Ananda not to give teachings in his absence. At that time, Ananda had not yet attained the miraculous power to travel to the Heaven of the Thirty-Three and therefore had to remain on earth. As a result, all teachings during that period were delivered through other means rather than being directly spoken by the Buddha.

MAIN BODY OF THE SUTRA

The actual main body of the Heart Sutra is divided into three main sub-headings:

1. Shariputra's query into the perfection of wisdom
2. Avalokiteshvara's response (presentation of the perfection of wisdom)
3. Affirmation and expression of rejoicing.

Shariputra's query into the perfection of wisdom:

"Thereupon, through the Buddha's inspiration, the venerable Shariputra spoke to the noble Avalokiteshvara, the bodhisattva, the great being, and said, "How should any noble son or nobledaughter who wishes to engage in the practice of the profound perfection of wisdom train?"

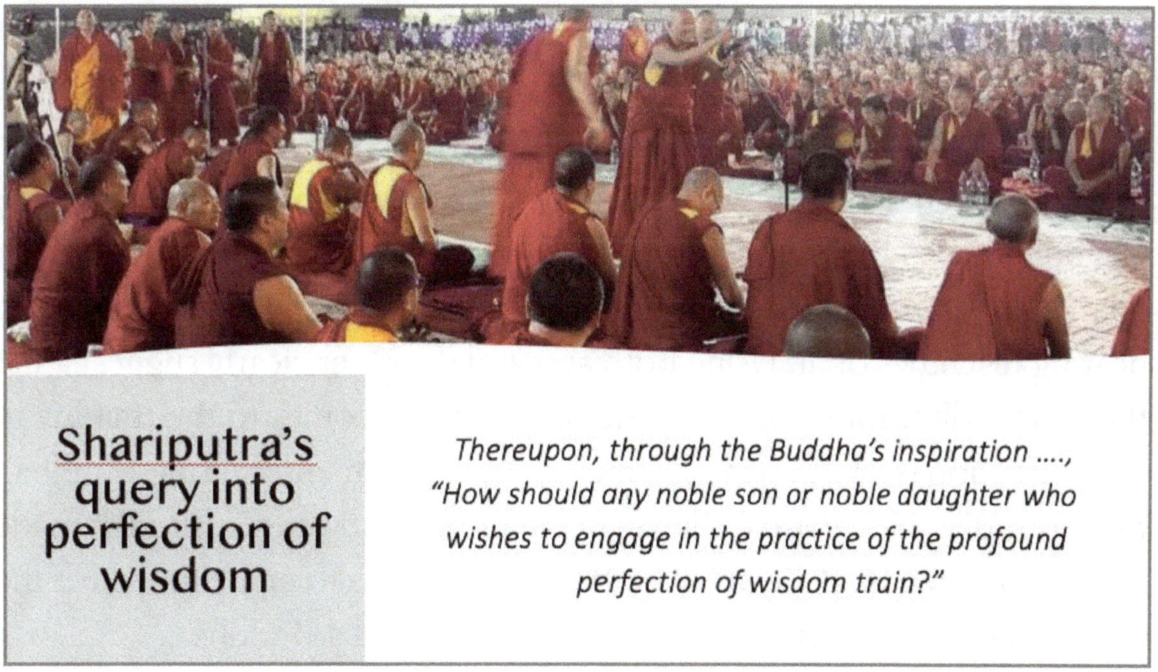

The question Shariputra put forth to Avalokiteshvara was: How should a noble son and a noble daughter should train in the practice of the profound perfection of wisdom? There is a reason behind the term noble son and noble daughter. From the Buddhist perspective, everyone, including tiny insects and serial killers, have the Buddha nature, the seed of pure potential to become enlightened. However, the seeds need to be nurtured and ripened in order to embark on the journey to enlightenment. A good analogy would be a piece of gold covered in mud. In terms of value and worth, there is no difference between a soiled piece of gold and a shiny one - it is simply a matter of cleaning off the dirt. Likewise, every ordinary being is akin to soiled gold. We all have the potential to become fully enlightened beings; it is just that at the moment, we are covered with thick layers of afflictive emotions. Through practice, we can gradually peel away these layers and eventually become completely free of all defilements. So here noble son and noble daughter refers to those in whom the Buddha nature has ripened. Those who were able to develop great compassion are considered to have ripened their Buddha nature.

There is another way to understand the term "noble son and noble daughter". Emptiness is not everyone's cup of tea. Not everyone is a suitable vessel to receive teachings on emptiness. Some develop extreme anxiety upon hearing emptiness. In that sense, noble son and noble daughter refers to those who are suited for the teachings on emptiness. Chandrakirti, in his *Entry into the Middle Way*, states that those with a deep connection to the topic of emptiness will naturally be moved to tears upon hearing teachings on it. Using both son and daughter clearly suggests that there is no discrimination or gender bias when it comes to the training in the perfection of wisdom and achieving enlightenment. During Buddha's time in India, there existed a strong gender bias and yet the Buddha made a clear statement that anyone whether male or female can be trained in the practice of the perfection of wisdom and become a Buddha.

Avalokiteshvara's response: The presentation of the perfection of wisdom and the Mahayana 5 Paths

"When this has been said, the holy Avalokiteshvara, the bodhisattva, the great being, spoke to the venerable Shariputra and said, "Shariputra, any noble son or noble daughter who wishes to engage in the practice of the profound perfection of wisdom should clearly see this way: they should see perfectly that even the five aggregates are empty of intrinsic existence….The mantra of the perfection of wisdom is proclaimed: tadyatha gate gate paragate parasamgate bodhi svaha!

Shariputra, the bodhisattvas, the great beings, should train in the perfection of wisdom in this way."

From here onwards Avalokiteshvara presents the method of engaging in the perfection of wisdom in two different ways: a detailed presentation for those who possess intelligence and a concise presentation for those who possess extraordinary intelligence. The detailed presentation covers the specific practices based on the stages of five paths. What are the Mahayana five paths?

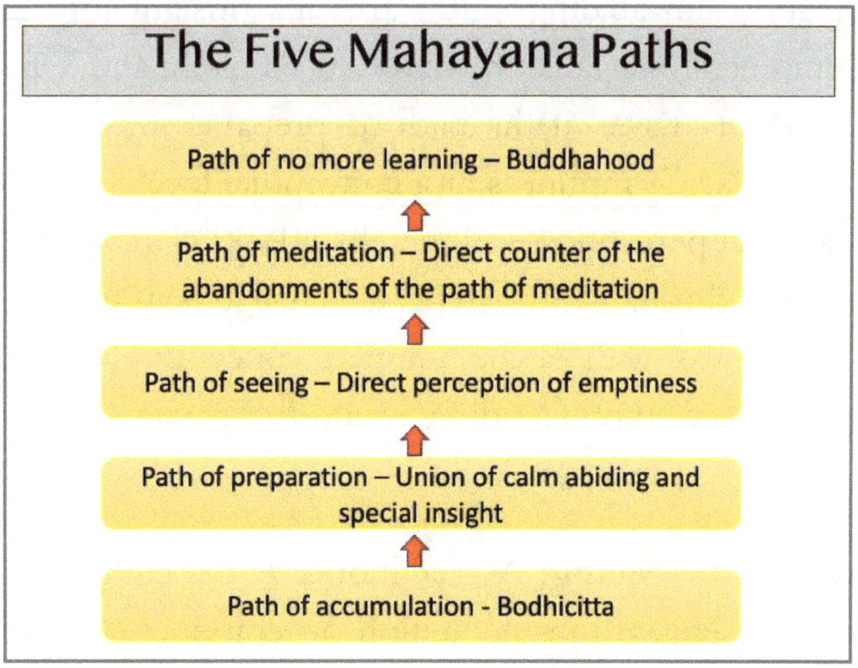

For a person to become buddha, one needs to "climb" the ladder of Mahayana five paths. In other words, one needs to cultivate the path to attain particular levels of realisations. These levels are like milestones of attainments as one progresses towards enlightenment: The path of accumulation, path of preparation, path of seeing, path of meditation and path of no more leaning.

(1) **The Path of Accumulation:** When a Mahayana practitioner first generates spontaneous, continuous bodhicitta (altruism), one enters the path of accumulation. By generating bodhicitta, one has begun to accumulate a mass of merits as from that moment, every practice will be motivated by bodhicitta thereby rendering every virtue enormously powerful. Hence this path is called the path of accumulation. However, at this stage, the practitioner may or may not have realized emptiness.

(2) **The Path of Preparation:** The practitioner who is at the path of accumulation, then engages in both single pointed meditation and insight meditation. Eventually, the person will achieve samadhi (calm abiding) and vipassana (insight into emptiness). The moment one gains the union of Samadhi and Vipassana, the practitioner arrives at the path of preparation. The practitioner can now "see" emptiness at a conceptual level. This however, is not a direct perception and thereby it lacks clarity. It is like seeing emptiness through a veil. Repeated engagement in the meditation on emptiness with single pointed concentration prepares the person to see emptiness directly and that's why this path is called the path of preparation.

(3) **The Path of Seeing:** A practitioner at the path of preparation repeatedly engages in meditation on emptiness and reaches the

point where one's understanding and realization of emptiness become so clear that it seems as though there is no distinction between emptiness and the mind that is cognizing it. When one finally gains such insight, one achieves the direct perception of emptiness and at this stage, attains the path of seeing and becomes an *arya* being.

(4) **The Path of Meditation**: Now equipped with direct perception into emptiness, the practitioner on the path of meditation continues to engage in meditation of emptiness to uproot the ignorance and its stains (subtle grasping at inherent existence/ grasp at the "I"/grasp at phenomena). These are the specific obscurations that the path of meditation has to counter are known as the "abandonments" of the path of meditation. From here until the complete eradication of these abandonments of the path of meditation (subtle grasping at inherent existence), is the path of meditation. Upon succeeding in eliminating the said abandonments, one enters the path of no more learning.

(5) **The Path of No More Learning:** This is where one becomes buddha. At this stage, one has abandoned all gross and subtle negativities and perfected all the qualities. This is the stage of omniscience or all-knowing and hence it is called the path of no more learning.

Training in the Path of Accumulation & Path of Preparation:

HEART SUTRA 2	When this had been said, the holy Avalokiteshvara, the bodhisattva, the great being, spoke to the venerable Shariputra and said, "Shariputra, any noble son or noble daughter who so wishes to engage in the practice of the profound perfection of wisdom should clearly see this way:

HEART SUTRA 3	they should see perfectly that even the five aggregates are empty of intrinsic existence." Form is empty, emptiness is form; emptiness is not other than form, form too is not other than emptiness. Likewise, feelings, perceptions, mental formations, and consciousness are all empty.

Avalokiteshvara begins his response by saying that whoever wishes to engage in the practice of the profound perfection of wisdom should clearly see even the five aggregates as empty of intrinsic existence. The word "even" emphasizes the importance of realizing the selflessness of the person ("person" refers to the concept or label "I") and as well as the selflessness of phenomena ("phenomena" refers to the aggregates). The rationale is that although we may intellectually understand or even perceive the emptiness of the person, as long as we hold onto the idea that the aggregates have an independent identity, the fault of self-grasping will exist. The belief in inherent existence is ignorance and living a life on that basis will inevitably leads to creating karma and thereby resulting in samsaric birth. Hence, realizing the selflessness of the person alone is not enough to escape samsara, let alone achieving the state of enlightenment. To elaborate his answer, Avalokiteshvara then says, "Form is empty, emptiness is form; emptiness is not other than form, form too is not other than emptiness."

Let's try to understand these four statements which is the core of Heart Sutra and known as the Fourfold approach to understanding emptiness. It is relatively easy to understand the first statement that form is emptiness. We have discussed how all things exist in dependence upon causes and conditions, component parts and mental imputation. If one's existence is dependent on something, by inference, it negates independent existence. This applies to form as well. The sutra called Questions of Anavatapta Sutra makes it clear when it says:

> "That which is born from condition is unborn,
> For it is devoid of intrinsic origination.
> That which depends upon conditions is declared empty.
> One who knows this emptiness remains tranquil."

So, Avalokiteshvara is saying that like everything else, form also is dependent on its causes and conditions and therefore it does not have independent existence. As such, form is empty of inherent existence. The form's mere lack of inherent existence is its emptiness. This applies to all phenomena. For example, a car lacks inherent nature and that is the car's emptiness. The car exists as a ***dependent arising*** (based on its parts, causes and conditions and mental labels) and does not exist as an independently, inherently existing car. The emptiness of car is nothing other than the car's ultimate nature. So, the mere absence of intrinsic nature of car is the car's ultimate nature or ultimate mode of being. In other words, the emptiness of car is one of the characteristics or one aspect of car.

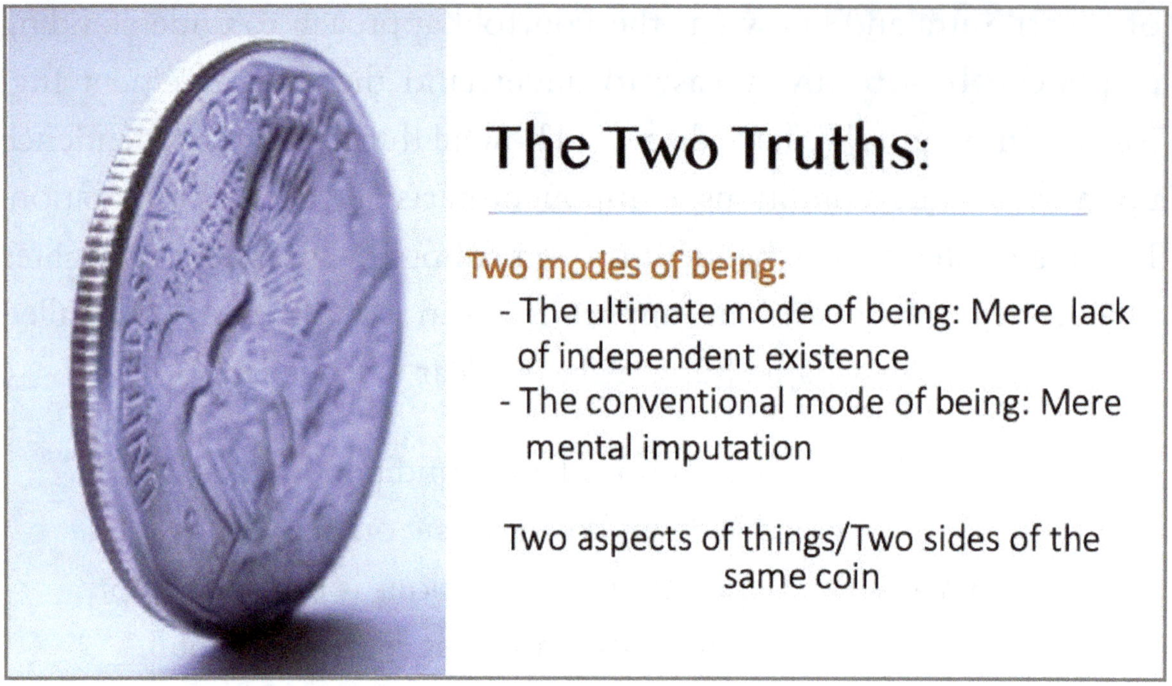

There is another aspect of form - its conventional mode of being. Although form does not exist inherently, it still exists. This existence is due to mental imputation. The form that is merely an imputation of the mind is the form's conventional truth or conventional mode of being. All things have these two modes of beings and it is commonly known as the two truths. The two modes of beings of form appear to be distinct but in reality they are the same. It is like the two sides of a coin.

The second statement says, "emptiness is form." What is form? Form is a mere imputation of mind onto a base; a label imputed on an aggregation of certain parts. A car for instance, is a label given to a combination of specific parts. This labeling or imputation is only tenable due to the fact that the car does not have independent existence. If a car had its own independent nature or identity, imputation by mind is not possible. In that sense, emptiness is the basis for the existence of car.

Look at the string knots in the picture. From one string, we can make all kinds of knots. This is only possible because of the string's malleability. If the string is hard and inflexible, making various shapes of knot is impossible. String's malleability serves as basis for all the conceivable types of knots. In that sense, all the various knots are like a manifestation of the string. Likewise, form is a manifestation of emptiness. Because things do not have inherent existence from their own side, varieties of forms can be perceived. In fact, all conventional things are manifestations or expressions of emptiness. Form being empty enables the existence of its convention aspect. Hence emptiness is form.

The third and fourth statement emphasizes the relationship between the two modes of being of a particular thing. These two modes of being appear to be distinct but in reality, they are the same. They are like the two sides of the coin. For instance, the ultimate nature of a car is emptiness which is the absence of intrinsic existence. Its conventional existence is nothing more than a label imputed on a base which is devoid of intrinsic existence.

The above fourfold approach to understanding emptiness should be applied to there maining four aggregates. Hence the text reads; "*likewise, feelings, perceptions, mental formations, and consciousness are all empty*". For instance, feeling is empty, emptiness is feeling, emptiness is not other than feeling, feeling too is not other than emptiness.

Training in the Path of Seeing

The text reads;

"Therefore, Shariputra, all phenomena are emptiness; they are without defining characteristics; they not born, they do not cease; they are not defiled, they are not undefiled, they are not deficient, and they are not complete".

This is to show how a person at the path of seeing should engage in the practice of perfection of wisdom. Avalokiteshvara advises that the person at this stage should engage in what is called the three doors of liberation, a way of examining emptiness from three different angles or perspectives.

The door of emptiness: The first way is examining emptiness from the point of view of emptiness itself. Avalokiteshvara says that as one has examined the five aggregates through the fourfold analysis, one should examine all phenomena in this way. When we do that, we will come to conclusion that all phenomena are emptiness. Even the defining characteristics of things are empty of inherent existence. At the conventional level, there exists defining characteristics - individual and common characteristics. However, at the ultimate level, there is no defining characteristics.

The door of signlessness: The second way of examining is looking at emptiness from the point of view of its **cause**. At the conventional level, the rise and fall, appearance and disappearance of things exists. There are origins of things and an end to things (again due to causes and conditions, parts and mental imputations coming together). However, because of this dependency of various factors, at the ultimate level, there is no independent origin nor cessation. Nothing is born inherently, and nothing ceases inherently. Likewise, the defilements that need to be abandoned and qualities that needs to be cultivated (such as liberation and Buddhahood) exist only as conventional reality. There is no inherent abandonment of defilements and cultivation of undefiled qualities.

The door of wishlessness: The third way is to examine emptiness from the point of view of its **effect.** At the conventional level, when we apply antidotes to afflictive emotions such as anger, attachment and ignorance, these afflictions will gradually diminish. Likewise, qualities such as compassion, kindness, patience can be developed and fully realized. As such, the diminution/decrease in negativities and increase in positive qualities exist. However, when we put them to ultimate analysis, these happen as products of dependencies and not inherently existing. Thus, nothing withstands ultimate analysis and therefore, all phenomena are empty of inherent existence.

Training in the Path of Meditation

To show how to train in the path of meditation, Avalokiteshvara continues;

"Therefore, Shariputra, in emptiness there is no form, no feelings, no perceptions, no mental formations, and no consciousness. There is no eye, no nose, no ear, no tongue, no body, and no mind. There is no form, no sound, no smell, no taste, no texture, and no mantal objects. There is no eye-element and so on up to no mind-element including up to no element of mental consciousness. There is no ignorance, there no extinction of ignorance and so on up to no aging and death and no extinction of aging and death. Likewise, there is no suffering, origin, cessation, or path; there is no wisdom, no attainment, and even no non-attainment."

In this statement, there are various categories of objects of investigation and hence we need to first unpack those. It begins with the five aggregates and the text negates each of them by saying there is no form, no feeling etc. The five aggregates do exist but what is being negated here is that it does not exist in the eyes of a practitioner who is at the path of meditation and is immersed in the meditation of emptiness. As practitioners at this level have already gained direct realization of emptiness, when they are in their meditative state, nothing other than emptiness (the mere absence of intrinsic nature) appears in their perceptions. Hence, in the eyes of such meditators, there are no forms, no feelings etc.

Following this, the text lists what is called the 18 elements, namely, the six elements of perceptual objects (visible forms, sound, smell, taste, tactile and phenomena), six elements of the sense faculties (eye sense faculty to mental sense faculty), and six elements of consciousness (eye consciousness to mental consciousness).

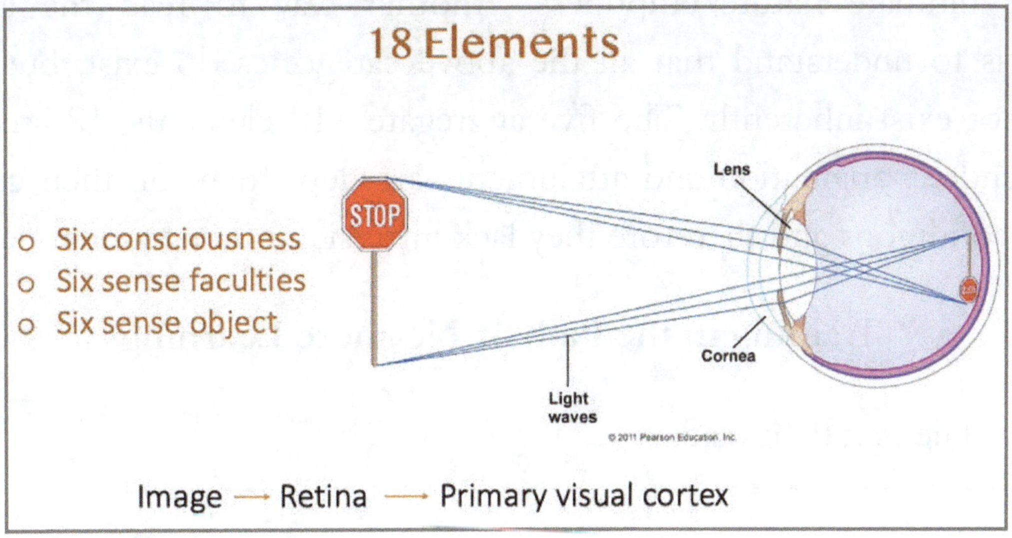

Avalokiteshvara says that all these 18 elements do not appear in the perception of such meditators who are absorbed in the meditation of emptiness. The 12 links of dependent origination, the four noble truths, wisdom, and attainments are another set of categories that are listed by Avalokiteshvara. Conventionally, the 12 links, the four noble truths and attainments exist but they are non-inherently existing to the eyes of a person who is immersed in a direct realization of emptiness. That's one way to read these lines as a way of training in the path of meditation.

12 Links of Dependent Origination

CATEGORY	LINK
Projecting Factors	(1) Ignorance (2) Compounded Karma (3) Consciousness
Actualizing Factors	(8) Craving (9) Grasping (10) Existence
Results	(4) Name & Form (5)Six sources (6) Contact (7) Feeling (11) Birth (12) Aging & death

As the path of meditation is a lengthy process, it requires constant and repeated engagement in the meditation of emptiness. To signify that, Avalokiteshvara listed numerous examples or objects to examine their ultimate nature/emptiness. Another way to read the above line is to understand that all the above categories do exist, but they do not exist inherently. The five aggregates, 18 elements, 12 links of dependent origination and attainments are dependent on their causes and conditions and therefore they lack intrinsic or independent nature.

Training in the Path of No-more Learning

The text then reads:

HEART SUTRA 5

> Therefore, Shariputra, since bodhsattvas have no attainments, they rely on this perfection of wisdom and abide in it. Having no obscuration in their minds, they have no fear, and by going utterly beyond error, they will reach the end of nirvana.

This segment falls under the training in the path of no more learning. In the first segment that reads; *"Therefore, Shariputra, since bodhisattvas have no attainments, they rely on this perfection of wisdom and abide in it"*, Avalokiteshvara says that the Bodhisattvas who have cognized the emptiness of all phenomena, including the final attainments, should immerse themselves in this direct realization of emptiness. This is the way to engage in the profound perfection of wisdom and hence they should abide in it. Avalokiteshvara then goes on to say that engaging in such way will eventually eliminate the self-grasping ignorance i.e. the grasping at the inherent existence of the person and of phenomena and thereby eradicate the two obscurations. As a result, there will be no more fear born out of self-grasping and instead go beyond the net of mistaken apprehension and reach the end of nirvana (Buddhahood). As states in the text, *"All the buddhas too who abide in the three times attained the full awakening of unexcelled, perfect enlightenment by relying on the profound perfection of wisdom"*- this is how all the Buddhas, the Buddhas of three times (past, present and future) achieve enlightenment, by engaging in and relying on the practice of the profound perfection of wisdom.

Concise presentation in the form of mantra

"Therefore, one should know that the mantra of the perfection of wisdom- the mantra of great knowledge, the unexcelled mantra, the mantra equal to the unequalled, the mantra that quells allsuffering-is true because it is not deceptive. The mantra of the perfection of wisdom is proclaimed:

Tadyatha gate gate paragate parasamgate bodhi svaha! Shariputra, the bodhsattvas, the greatbeings, should train in the perfection of wisdom in this way."

Up to this point, Avalokiteshvara presents the explanation of emptiness in a detailed manner mainly for those practitioners who are of intelligence. Now Avalokiteshvara turns to those who are of extraordinary intelligence and delivers a concise presentation in the form of mantra. It first extolls the perfection of wisdom. The text reads; *"Therefore, one should know that the mantra of the perfection of wisdom - the mantra of great knowledge … because it is not deceptive."* The perfection of wisdom is called the mantra because it enables a person to cross the ocean of samsara. This also aligns with the etymological meaning of mantra which is "to protect the mind". Wisdom realizing emptiness safeguards one from self-grasping ignorance. It is called the mantra of great knowledge because it overcomes all forms of ignorance and resultant afflictive emotions. It is also known as unexcelled mantra because there is no other path that excels the perfection of wisdom in terms of leading to the state of enlightenment. It is called the mantra equal to the unequal because the perfection of wisdom enables one to achieve the state equal to Buddha state which is unequalled. The perfection of wisdom is like a panacea to all sufferings and its causes and thereby it is called the mantra that quells all suffering. The perfection of wisdom perceives the ultimate reality of things and there is no disparity between appearance and reality. Therefore, it is true and not deceptive.

The actual mantra is TADYATHA GATE GATE PARAGATE PARASAMGATEBODHI SVAHA

Generally, the Perfection of Wisdom sutras have an explicit subject (emptiness) and an implicit subject (stages of the path associated with the wisdom realizing emptiness). The above mantra brings forth the implicit subject matter of Heart sutra and is in Sanskrit. *Tadyatha* means "it is thus" or "it is like this". *Gate Gate* means "go, go"; *Paragate* means "go beyond"; *Parasamagate* means "go totally beyond"; and *Bodhi Svaha* means "be rooted in the ground of enlightenment." Put all this together becomes "Go, go, go beyond, go totally beyond, be rooted in the ground of enlightenment." This may still not make much sense. However, if we bring it in relation to the five paths, it will make more sense. Avalokiteshvara urges practitioner to engage in the five paths: The first and the second "Go", calls for the trainee to enter the path of accumulation and path of preparation respectively. "Go beyond" and "Go totally beyond" are exhortation to enter the path of seeing and path of meditation respectively. Finally, "Bodhi Svaha" is an exhortation to enter the final path, the state of no more learning, of enlightenment. This lays out the stages of paths that one gradually needs to ascend in order to reach Buddhahood, the full emancipation. Avalokiteshvara affirms to Shariputra that thisis the way to engage in the practice of perfection of wisdom as the text reads; *"Shariputra, the bodhisattvas, the great beings, should train in the perfection of wisdom in this way."* This concludes Avalokiteshvara's answer to the question put forth by Shariputra.

CONCLUSION

Affirmation and expression of rejoicing

The text then reads;

"Thereupon, the Blessed One arose from that meditative absorption and commented the holy Avalokiteshvara, the bodhisattva, the great being, saying this is excellent. Excellent! Excellent! O noble child, it is just so; it should be just so. One must practice the profound perfection of wisdom just as you have revealed. For then even the tathagatas will rejoice".

Up to this point, throughout the dialogue between Shariputra and Avalokiteshvara, Buddha was absorbed in meditation. At this point, Buddha arose from his meditative state to commend and affirm Avalokiteshvara's presentation on the perfection of wisdom by saying *"Excellent! Excellent! O noble child, it is just so; it should be just so. One must practice the profound perfection of wisdom just as you have revealed. For then even the tathagatas will rejoice."* This segment of the Heart Sutra falls under the category of teachings that are spoken by the Buddha himself.

The final part of the Heart Sutra is about how the audience expressed theirrejoicing. The text reads;

"As the Blessed One uttered these words, the venerable Shariputra, the holy Avalokiteshvara, thebodhisattva, the great being, along with the entire assembly, including the worlds of gods, humans,asuras, and gandhavaras, all rejoiced and hailed what the Blessed One had said."

Thereafter Buddha gave his compliments to Avalokiteshvara, all who were present at the gathering including the worlds of gods, humans, asuras, and gandharvas, expressed their rejoice and hailed the

Buddha for giving this precious teaching.

Final Words & Dedication

The *Heart Sutra* is profound and we've already explored many of its benefits. Now, we need to apply that understanding - one way is through analytical meditation.

For those who engage in some form of daily spiritual practice, before beginning your session, take a few moments to do a simple meditation using this analysis derived from these verses composed by Nagarjuna:

"A person is not earth, not water,
Not fire, not wind, not space,
Nor consciousness, and all of them.
What person is there other than these?

Just as a person is not real
Due to being a composite of six constituents,
So, each of the constituents also
Is not real due to being composite."

These verses guide us in meditating on the emptiness of the person and of phenomena. Begin by generating a strong sense of "I." You can use any method that helps evoke this feeling-recall an upsetting event that triggered your anger, such as someone insulting you.

Once this vivid sense of self arises, observe how it appears. Usually, this "I" feels very solid, independent - something that seems to exist on its own, without relyingon anything else. If it appears that way - as truly existing-then we need toexamine it further.

We ask: *Where is this "I"?* We must search for this seemingly solid "I." The reasoning is: if something exists inherently, it should be findable - we should be able to point to it and say, "There it is."

So, return to Nagarjuna's verse: "A person is not earth, not water…" Look first at the solid parts of your body-are they the "I"? What about the liquid parts, the water element - are they "me"? When we go through each part and eliminate them one by one, we arrive at the conclusion that none - not even a single atom-is the "I." Then we examine the mind, consciousness - are any of those the self? Is the hand "I"? Is the head "I"? No.

Through this process of elimination, we may come to a realization: "Oh, there is no truly existing 'I'." At a recent online teaching, His Holiness shared that when Holiness had this realization, it brought on a certain fear, "Oh, there is no 'I'!" But Holiness said this fear is a good sign - it reflects some experiential understanding of emptiness. When we reach this conclusion, we mentally remain in the void that arises from negating the inherently existing "I." Try to abide in that state of awareness of emptiness as long as possible.

However, it's crucial to understand: though we negate a *truly existing* "I," we do not deny the existence of "I" or "self." We are not saying there is no self at all. What we realize is that the self doesn't exist in the solid, independent way we perceive. Instead, the "I" exists in dependence upon its basis - the aggregates. The "I" is a label we impute onto the collection of aggregates. This might give the impression that while the "I" lacks inherent existence, its basis - the aggregates - exist inherently. To counter that, we contemplate on the second verse:

"Just as a person is not real

Due to being a composite of six constituents,
So, each of the constituents also
Is not real due to being composite."

Just as the person isn't ultimately self - existing or real due to being a composite (a collection of parts and labels), each of the six constituents is also not inherently existent. Through this analysis, we realize that even the aggregates-form, feeling, perception, formation, consciousness, and so on-are empty of inherent existence.

Again, try to remain in that state of awareness of voidness for as long as you can. Eventually, we come to the realization that all things, including the self, are dependently arisen. The "I" is merely a label applied to a collection of parts - just like a chariot is a name we assign to an arrangement of wheels, axles, and components. So, the person is not inherently real, and neither are the parts. The person exists in dependence on its causes, conditions, parts and labelling.

What I've shared here is only the tip of the iceberg. This is an introduction to the *Heart Sutra.* This profound text can be studied and taught at many levels. What I've offered is just a beginning. So don't stop here. Continue studying and reflecting deeply on this topic.

Always remember emptiness. Keep that awareness with you in all that you do. It will be especially helpful in your daily interactions. All our discriminations and afflictions arise from misapprehension - our mistaken belief in solid, inherently existing things. We see enemies and problems as self-existing. We see things as fixed and real, not as mental constructions. But if we can recognize that things are merely labelled by the mind, as mere imputations onto a base, our grasping will begin to loosen. Our tight grip on things will start to ease. And with that, peace will gradually arise within us. All the best.

Due to this virtue, may all beings
Complete the merits of virtue and wisdom,
And attain the two holy bodies
That arise from [the merits of] virtue and wisdom.

ABOUT THE AUTHOR

Drupa Rinpoche (Lobsang Yeshi) is a Tibetan Buddhist monk and is 7th in the lineage of Drupa Rinpoches. Rinpoche was born in India and in 1988, was recognized by His Holiness the 14th Dalai Lama as the reincarnation of the 6th Drupa Rinpoche Shedrup Tenpai Gyaltsen. Rinpoche is the head of Drupa Monastery in Kham, Eastern Tibet.

Rinpoche holds a monastic Geshe degree in Buddhist philosophy from Drepung Loselling Monastery (South India), a B. Psychology (HELP University, Malaysia) and an M.Sc in Positive Psychology (Life University, Georgia, USA). He is the resident teacher at Kachoeling Dharma Center in Minneapolis and also the founder of the non-profit organisation named Drupa Monastery Oasis of Dharma in Saint Paul, Minnesota. Rinpoche worked as a researcher at the University of Minnesota's School of Public Health and is a volunteer Buddhist Chaplain at the Hennepin County Medical Center.

ROOT TEXT

Heart Sutra
(The Sutra of the Heart of Transcendent Knowledge)

Homage to the Bhagavatī Prajñāpāramitā!

Thus have I heard. At one time the Blessed One was dwelling in Rājgṛha at Vulture Peak mountain, together with a great community of monks and a great community of bodhisattvas.

At that time, the Blessed One entered an absorption on categories of phenomena called 'perception of the profound'. At the same time, noble Avalokiteśvara, the bodhisattva and great being, beheld the practice of the profound perfection of wisdom, and saw that the five aggregatesare empty of nature. Then, through the Buddha's power, venerable Śāriputra said to noble Avalokiteśvara, the bodhisattva and great being: "How should a child of noble family who wishes to practise the profound perfection of wisdom train?"

This is what he said, and the noble Avalokiteśvara, the bodhisattva and great being, replied to venerable Śāriputra as follows: "O Śāriputra, a son of noble family or daughter of noble family who wishes to practise the profound perfection of wisdom should regard things in this way: they should see the five aggregates to be empty of nature. Form is empty; emptiness is form. Emptiness is not other than form; form is not other than emptiness. In the same way, sensation, recognition, conditioning factors, and consciousness are emptiness.

Therefore, Śāriputra, all dharmas are emptiness; they are without characteristics; they are unarisen and unceasing; they are not tainted and not untainted; they are not deficient and not complete. Therefore, Śāriputra, in emptiness, there is no form, no sensation, no recognition, no conditioning factors, no consciousness; no eye, no ear, no nose, no tongue, no body, no mind; no visible form, no sound, no odour, no taste, no texture and no mental objects; there is no eye element up to no mind element and as far as no mental consciousness element; there is no ignorance, no extinction of ignorance up to no old age and death, no extinction of old age and death.

Likewise, there is no suffering, no origin, no cessation and no path, no wisdom, no attainment, and no non-attainment. Therefore, Śāriputra, since bodhisattvas haveno attainment, they rely on and abide by the perfection of wisdom. Since their minds are unobscured, they have no fear. They completely transcend error and reach the ultimate nirvāṇa. All the buddhas throughout the three times fully awaken to unsurpassed, genuine and complete enlightenment by means of the perfection of wisdom. Therefore, the mantra of the perfection of wisdom-the mantra of great insight, the unsurpassed mantra, the mantra that equals the unequalled, the mantra that pacifies all suffering-is not false and should thus be understood as true. The mantra of the perfection of wisdom is proclaimed as follows:

[oṃ] gate gate pāragate pārasaṃgate bodhisvāhā.

Śāriputra, a bodhisattva and great being should train in the profound perfection of wisdom in this way."

Thereupon, the Blessed One arose from that absorption and commended Avalokiteśvara, the bodhisattva and great being: "Excellent, excellent indeed, O son of noble family, that is how it is. That is just how it is. One should practise the profound perfection of wisdom just as you have taught and then even the tathāgatas will rejoice."

When the Blessed One had said this, venerable Śāriputra, and noble Avalokiteśvara, the bodhisattva and great being, together with the whole assembly and the world of gods, human beings, *asuras* and *gandharvas* rejoiced and praised the speech of the Blessed One.

MỤC LỤC

LỜI TÁC GIẢ

Nội dung cuốn sách này được trích từ các bản ghi chép giảng dạy trong lớp Pháp về Bát Nhã Tâm Kinh mà tôi đã thuyết giảng tại Trung tâm Khacholing, Minneapolis, Minnesota. Những hình ảnh kèm theo là một số slide được sử dụng trong buổi học. Khi nhận được sự góp ý và thỉnh cầu xuất bản các bản ghi chép thành sách, nhằm hỗ trợ những người đang tìm kiếm nền tảng nhập môn về chủ đề thâm sâu của tính Không, tôi đã khởi sự công việc này.

Việc xuất bản cuốn sách song ngữ này thành hiện thực là nhờ sự bảo trợ rộng lượng của bà Nguyễn Thị Ngọc Nga – một hành giả Phật pháp chân thành, luôn nhiệt tâm ủng hộ các công việc hoằng dương Giáo pháp. Chính bà cũng đã sắp xếp để cuốn sách được dịch sang tiếng Việt bởi Nga-kpa Kunga Lodro Thịnh Nguyễn. Tôi cũng xin trân trọng tri ân sự giúp đỡ của bà Yeo Puay Huei, người đã khích lệ tôi thực hiện cuốn sách này và hỗ trợ trong việc hiệu đính.

Mọi sai sót trong sách đều hoàn toàn thuộc về tôi, và tôi xin thành tâm sám hối. Dù vậy, cuốn sách này được gửi gắm với lời cầu nguyện tha thiết: mong rằng ít nhất có thể đem lại cho một người nào đó chút hiểu biết về tính Không, soi sáng phần nào con đường giác ngộ, và mang lại chút an ủi, vơi bớt khổ đau trong biển khổ luân hồi.

Drupa Rinpoche

Hòa Thượng Thích Quảng Tùng

LỜI GIỚI THIỆU

Bát-nhã Tâm Kinh là một trong các bộ kinh đặc biệt quan trọng trong Phật giáo Đại thừa cũng như Kim Cang thừa. Là hành giả Đại thừa nhiều năm công phu nghiên cứu và hành trì giáo nghĩa, tinh yếu của các bản *kinh Hoa Nghiêm, Viên Giác, Lăng Nghiêm, Pháp Hoa, Lăng Già, Bát Nhã*... tôi rất tâm đắc và hoan hỷ với tác phẩm này của tác giả Ngài Drupa Rinpoche (Lobsang Yeshi); tán thán công đức dịch của dịch giả Việt Nam (chú Thịnh) – nhân duyên ban dịch thuật Trung Tâm Phật học ứng dụng Việt Nam.

Tại Tây Tạng, kinh điển thường được in khắc gỗ. Đức Phật thuyết Pháp tại nhiều nơi, nhưng trong suốt thời gian tại thế, không có lời dạy nào được ghi chép thành văn bản. Tất cả đều được truyền thừa bằng khẩu truyền. Sau khi Ngài nhập Niết-bàn, các đại hội kết tập kinh điển được tổ chức, các vị đệ tử xuất sắc đã ghi nhớ lời dạy của Ngài - cùng nhau tụng đọc lại các pháp thoại, và từ đó mới được chép lại thành văn; là những hành giả có công phu thiền định thâm sâu và trí nhớ phi thường, nhờ đó có thể ghi nhớ lời Phật dạy với sự minh bạch và chính xác cao độ; có một truyền thuyết kể rằng, sau khi Đức Phật nhập diệt, chư thiên, a-tu-la và long vương đã tụ hội để bàn luận xem ai sẽ là vị giữ gìn những giáo pháp. Vì không thể đi đến đồng thuận, các bản kinh được cho là đã bị phân tán khắp mọi phương. Một truyền thuyết cho rằng các bộ *kinh Bát-nhã ba-la-mật* đã được Long tộc (Nāga) gìn giữ. Về sau, Bồ-tát Long Thọ (Nāgārjuna) đã đến cõi Long tộc và thỉnh các bản kinh ấy; Long tộc không trao trả toàn bộ các phẩm kinh, mà giữ lại một số chương nhằm khuyến khích Long Thọ quay lại. Do vậy, trong một số bản *kinh Bát-nhã ba-la-mật*, có những phẩm bị khuyết lạc. Những đoạn trích lịch sử Phật giáo mà tác phẩm đưa ra, chúng tôi tán thán; vì ở các quốc độ khác nhau, nhưng cùng được nghiên cứu giáo lý chung của Đức Phật, được công lao các dịch giả chuyển ngữ, chúng tôi – những hành giả đồng thời là học giả được nghiên cứu hệ thống kinh điển của các truyền thống đều có tri nhận và cách tiếp cận chung.

Tác phẩm của Ngài Drupa Rinpoche (Lobsang Yeshi) trước khi đi sâu vào *Bát-nhã Tâm Kinh*, đã chỉ ra bốn tông phái chính trong Phật giáo và quan điểm của họ về vô ngã: *Tông Hữu bộ (Vaibhāṣika), Tông Kinh lượng bộ (Sautrāntika), Tông Duy thức (Cittamātra), Tông Trung quán (Mādhyamika)* (Tông Tự lập Trung quán (Svātantrika) và Tông Y tha khởi Trung quán (Prāsaṅgika)). Hai tông đầu, không luận giải về vô ngã của chư pháp; hai tông sau, khẳng định vô ngã của chư pháp, nhắm đến giác ngộ viên mãn (Phật quả), luận về hai tầng chướng ngại cần đoạn trừ để thành tựu giác ngộ viên mãn: Phiền não chướng (kleśa-āvaraṇa) như tham, sân, si - Sở tri chướng (jñeya-āvaraṇa), chướng ngại nhận thức, vọng tưởng, tà kiến, chướng ngại cho trí tuệ toàn giác (nhất thiết trí); để đoạn trừ sở tri chướng, cần chứng ngộ Không chỉ vô ngã của ngã thể, vô ngã của chư pháp - tức là thấy rõ tất cả hiện tượng đều không có tự tính, chỉ tồn tại do duyên khởi và quy ước. Đặc biệt, Vô ngã và Duyên khởi - Trung quán Cụ duyên (Prāsaṅgika Madhyamika) - được xem là tối thượng, cho rằng không pháp nào hiện hữu từ tự thân; ba tông phái còn lại quan điểm cần phải có một thực thể hiện hữu nội tại làm nền tảng cho sự gán danh. Prāsaṅgika chủ trương ngay cả nền tảng để thiết lập danh xưng cũng không hiện hữu một cách tự tính. Mọi pháp đều rỗng không về tự tính. Điều này trở nên đặc biệt quan trọng khi quán chiếu *Bát-nhã Tâm Kinh*. Cả bốn tông đều khẳng định quan điểm của Phật giáo là không có một "ngã" nào tồn tại độc lập với các uẩn; "ngã" nương vào ngũ uẩn mà hiện khởi - chỉ là một giả danh quy ước do tâm phân biệt gán đặt.

Bát-nhã Tâm Kinh có thể coi như bản kinh gối đầu giường của Tăng Ni Phật tử Đại thừa, rất nổi tiếng. Đối với người Tây Tạng cũng như Đại thừa Việt Nam, thường được trì tụng hằng ngày tại các thiền viện và tư gia. Bản kinh tuy ngắn, liên quan tính Không chân đế vượt ngoài các tướng chấp ngôn ngữ thông thường, người đắc Pháp cũng "tâm truyền tâm bất lập văn tự", ngoài ngôn thuyết; vì vậy ý nghĩa sâu vi diệu không phải hành giả nào cũng lĩnh hội được yếu chỉ - hiểu đúng đắn về tính Không tường tận. Chính vì vậy, từ quá khứ đến hiện đại, rất nhiều các luận Sư, nhà khoa học luận giải về Tính Không, bàn về Bát nhã, triết lý các kinh điển Đại thừa rất nhiều, bất khả tư nghì, nhưng không bao giờ bàn hết; đó là cái uyên áo sâu thẳm rộng lớn không ngằn mé của giáo Pháp Đại thừa mà chỉ những hành giả thực chứng trực nhận truyền thừa. Cũng như tác giả Ngài Drupa Rinpoche (Lobsang Yeshi) dù rất thông tuệ cả Pháp học và Pháp hành bài bản nhưng đã nói "khiêm tốn" trong cuốn sách này: "Tôi không thể đi sâu vào đề tài này đến mức ấy. Tôi không có đủ tuệ giác hay năng lực để trình bày một cách thật chi tiết. Vì thế, thật đáng tiếc cho quý vị - quý vị lại gặp tôi để giúp hiểu phần nào về bản kinh này. Tuy nhiên, tôi vẫn sẽ cố gắng lần lượt đi qua từng câu trong kinh và đưa ra một vài lời giải thích. Trong tiếng Tây Tạng, cách trình bày này gọi là *tsig-'drel*, tức là giải thích từng từ hoặc từng cụm từ". Tác phẩm đã khéo nhắc nhở, do "cảm nhận sai lầm về "ngã". Chúng ta đã kiến lập một ý niệm tinh vi về một cái "ngã" kiên cố, có thật. Nhưng thực chất, không hề có một cái "ngã" hiện hữu tự tính. Chỉ có một khái niệm về "ngã" được gán đặt lên ngũ uẩn (sắc và tâm) mà thôi. Thế mà chúng ta lại khổ đau và lao nhọc vì cái "ngã" hư vọng ấy". Đây chính là tinh yếu của *Bát-nhã Tâm Kinh - Tâm Kinh*, tinh túy của toàn bộ giáo pháp *Bát-nhã ba-la-mật* về Tính Không. Tôi xin trân trọng giới thiệu đến quý Trưởng lão Tăng Ni Đại Đức, nhà khoa học, quý độc giả Quốc tê.

Việt Nam ngày 8 tháng 8 năm 2025

Hòa Thượng Thích Quảng Tùng

Phó Chủ Tịch Hội Đồng Trị Sự Trung Ương Giáo Hội Phật Giáo Việt Nam

Trưởng Ban Từ Thiện Trung Ương Giáo Hội Phật Giáo Việt Nam

Trưởng Ban Trị Sự Giáo Hội Phật Giáo Việt Nam tỉnh Hải Phòng

Thiền sư Ottamathara

LỜI GIỚI THIỆU

Đức Phật dạy trong *Kinh Tăng Chi Bộ III, chương Tám Pháp, phẩm Lớn*: "Ví như nước biển chỉ có một vị là vị mặn, cũng vậy, này Pahàrada, Pháp và Luật của Ta chỉ có một vị là vị giải thoát". Đối tượng giảng dạy chính của Đức Phật là con người trong thế giới này.

Từ thời Phật tại thế, sự phân chia hệ phái đã manh nha, Phật giáo hiện nay có ba phái chính là Nguyên thủy, Đại thừa, Kim Cang thừa, và hàng trăm hành ngàn các tông môn, sơn môn của các hệ phái. Nhưng xét một cách căn bản về giáo lý – các Pháp số căn bản không có sự sai khác; mỗi truyền thống giáo lý đều đưa ra các đạo lộ tu tập cho hành giả mục đích giải thoát sanh tử luân hồi, nhận thức được đâu là thiện đâu là bất thiện, để chuyển mê khai ngộ chuyển phàm thành Thánh. Thấy rõ, chính hành vi (nghiệp/kamma) dẫn chúng sinh luân hồi vào ba cõi: Dục giới, Sắc giới và Vô sắc giới; chứ không có sự sai khác về chân lý; Đức Phật chỉ là người khám phá ra chân lý, dù Phật Ngài có ra đời hay không thì chân lý vẫn tồn tại như vậy. Đức Phật có đầy đủ các parami nhiều đời nhiều kiếp tu hành công hạnh để trở thành bậc Vô Thượng Chánh Đẳng Chánh Giác với 10 hiệu, Thầy của Trời người, cao quý tột cùng, Pháp Ngài khai sáng không Thầy chỉ dạy "Thiên thượng thiên hạ duy ngã độc tôn", trên trời dưới trời không ai cao bằng Phật; khó khăn lắm mới có một vị Phật toàn giác xuất hiện trong nhân thế chỉ bày con đường Thánh Qủa cho chúng sanh. Vì vậy, trên 20 năm dạy Thiền Vipassana và thành lập hệ thống các trường Thiền mang tên Thabarwa tại Myanmar và cả phương Đông, phương Tây, chúng tôi luôn nhấn mạnh Pháp Hành. Bởi chỉ có hành trì và kiểm nghiệm Pháp chúng ta mới có tiếng nói chung mà không phải sự hý luận hay quan điểm chấp chặt trong ý thức tư tưởng của ngã chấp đánh lừa; chính vì thế tôi luôn dạy cho học trò mình nhấn mạnh "sự thật tục đế", sự thật của vạn pháp vận hành theo nguyên lý Nhân – Duyên – Qủa (Nhân Quả); và với những hành giả/ thiền sinh nặng về chấp dính, tôi luôn dạy bước đầu "làm thiện pháp không giới hạn/ làm thiện pháp một cách miên mật/ chỉ làm và làm mà thôi – thân và tâm này chỉ để sử dụng", vì con người khó làm điều lành hơn làm các bất thiện của thân – miệng – ý nên tôi luôn dạy học trò cần làm các điều thiện nhiều hơn như chúng sanh đang dễ duôi theo ác nghiệp. Cũng như trong tác phẩm này của Ngài Drupa Rinpoche (Lobsang Yeshi) đã chỉ ra: Chúng sinh thuộc *Dục giới* (bao gồm cõi người) đuổi theo các dục lạc cảm quan. Chúng sinh *Sắc giới* đã vượt qua dục ái thô thiển, thay vào đó tìm cầu lạc thọ phát sinh từ thiền định, rốt ráo hướng đến xả thọ (cảm giác trung tính). Chúng sinh thuộc *Vô sắc g*iới lìa bỏ toàn bộ sắc pháp, chỉ còn an trụ nơi tâm, rồi tuần tự tiến vào các tầng thiền định vi tế: *hư không vô biên xứ, thức vô biên xứ, vô sở hữu xứ*, và sau cùng là *phi tưởng phi phi tưởng* xứ. Nhiều tông phái phi Phật giáo tại Ấn Độ xem các tầng thiền định này là cứu cánh tối hậu - tức giải thoát. Tuy nhiên, theo quan điểm của Phật giáo, chừng nào các tầng định ấy không được phối hợp với trí tuệ quán chiếu tánh Không/ các pháp hữu vi duyên hợp giả tạm không thực thể/ Vipassana, thì hành giả vẫn bị vô minh chi phối, vẫn còn trầm luân trong luân hồi sinh tử, và vì thế vẫn phải chịu khổ.

Phật Ngài đã thấy rõ hai loại chấp thủ: chấp ngã (chấp vào một tự ngã hiện hữu thật) và chấp pháp (chấp các pháp là có tự tính hiện thực) - căn nguyên của ái (tham luyến), nguồn gốc của khổ đau. Vì vậy, các Trung

Tâm thiền Thabarwa bên cạnh việc hành Thiền Vipassana đòi hỏi hành giả phải quán chiếu thân tâm 24/24 trong các oai nghi, thấy rõ sự sanh diệt vô thường, trùng trùng duyên khởi không thực tướng để buông bỏ; từ đó chúng tôi "tự nhiên" trong hoàn cảnh chính trị bất ổn nội chiến của Myanmar trong nhiều năm qua "an sinh phúc lợi xã hội" thiết thực giúp được nhiều người nương tựa, gieo duyên cho họ gắn bó sâu sắc hơn với Phật Pháp Tăng; do đó Thabarwa tiếp nhận tất cả mọi cảnh đời: người già, người bệnh hiểm nghèo, người không nơi nương tựa, mẹ đơn thân, trẻ em mồ côi, cả người tâm thần, HIV-AIDS,...; chúng tôi còn tích cực bảo vệ môi trường, tái chế rác thải, kêu gọi hòa bình ngừng bắn/ngừng tranh chấp; đó cũng chính là những điểm tương đồng với Phật giáo Đại thừa, lý tưởng Bồ-tát hạnh, Tứ vô lượng tâm (Từ, Bi, Hỷ, Xả), Tứ nhiếp pháp (Bố thí, ái ngữ, lợi hành, đồng sự).

Bát-nhã Tâm Kinh là bản kinh rất nổi tiếng, từ lâu đã được dịch sang tiếng Anh, sự hiểu biết về tánh Không cũng như quan điểm vô chấp, vô trụ, chánh niệm xả ly, hướng đến "Sự Thật Chân Đế", là Như Lai Tạng, Tánh Biết trong Thiền Vipassana. Thời hiện đại, ở Thái Lan, thiền sư Ajahn chah, Việt Nam có Hòa thượng Thích Viên Minh – chùa Bửu Long, Thành phố Hồ Chí Minh, tôi nghĩ các vị ấy tu theo truyền thống Nguyên thủy Phật giáo nhưng quý Ngài hiểu sâu sắc về Tánh Không Duyên Khởi. Cuốn sách này của Ngài Drupa Rinpoche (Lobsang Yeshi) góp phần phát triển Phật giáo Quốc Tế nói chung trong tinh thần từ bi vô ngã, Trung đạo, giác ngộ giải thoát sanh tử luân hồi, vì hòa bình tiến bộ bền vững của nhân loại như Vesak 2025 Liên Hợp Quốc đưa ra. Tôi tán thán tinh thần phụng sự của Ngài Drupa Rinpoche (Lobsang Yeshi) cũng như trân trọng sâu sắc giáo lý Tánh Không như *Kinh Bát nhã* đã đưa ra để các hành giả và nhân loại phát triển lòng bi mẫn, chung tay vì một thế giới tốt đẹp, góp phần lan tỏa các giá trị ứng dụng của Phật học.

Mỹ Quốc, ngày 10 tháng 8 năm 2025

Thiền sư Ottamathara

Viện chủ sáng lập trên 125 trường thiền mang tên Thabarwa Quốc tế

Tiến sĩ Triết học Mexico

Tiến sĩ Danh Dự Ấn Độ

Ban Quốc tế - Trung Tâm Phật học ứng dụng Việt Nam

Phó giáo sư – Tiến sĩ
Quách Cơ Thụy Frank, J.R. GUO

LỜI GIỚI THIỆU

Bát-nhã Tâm Kinh -Tinh yếu của Kinh Bát-nhã Ba-la-mật-đa. Tác phẩm đã đưa ra, theo quan điểm Đại thừa, Đức Phật giảng vô lượng giáo pháp - tám vạn bốn nghìn pháp môn/pháp tạng/pháp uẩn; trình bày qua từng giai đoạn, là Ba lần Chuyển bánh xe Chánh Pháp. (1) *Lần Chuyển bánh xe Chánh Pháp thứ nhất* tập trung vào giáo lý *Tứ Diệu Đế.* (2) *Lần Chuyển thứ hai* trình bày giáo pháp về *Bát-nhã Ba-la-mật-đa* (tánh Không). (3) *Lần Chuyển thứ ba* làm rõ những lời dạy của Đức Phật về tánh Không. *Bát-nhã Tâm Kinh* thuộc về hệ thống giáo pháp về tánh Không, được tuyên thuyết trong *Lần Chuyển bánh xe Chánh Pháp thứ hai.* Sau khi chứng đắc Vô thượng Bồ-đề, Đức Phật ban đầu giữ im lặng, vì những điều Ngài giác ngộ quá khó để người bình thường có thể tin hiểu lĩnh hội; khi Thiên Chủ Đế Thích (Śakra) cầu thỉnh Ngài mới bắt đầu chuyển pháp luân, bài đầu tiên tại Lộc Uyển (*Sarnath*) là Tứ Diệu Đế. Trong đó, vấn đề dẹp vọng tưởng và phiền não bằng con đường *Đạo đế - c*on đường tối hậu với tuệ quán chính là quán chiếu Tánh Không (gắn liền *Duyên khởi*), Ngài Long Thọ (*Nāgārjuna*) đã có công thúc đẩy Tánh Không lên đỉnh điểm qua tác phẩm *Trung Quán Luận.*

Tác phẩm này, Ngài Drupa Rinpoche (Lobsang Yeshi) cũng dẫn ra lời Tổ Tông-khách-ba (*Tsongkhapa*), trong *Luận ba yếu tố chính của đạo lộ*: "Nếu không có trí tuệ chứng ngộ thực tại tối hậu, thì dù có phát khởi tâm xả ly và Bồ-đề tâm, cũng không thể đoạn trừ tận gốc luân hồi sinh tử". Tức nếu không có tuệ giác quán chiếu tánh Không, thì không có con đường nào có thể đoạn trừ khổ đau tận gốc. Ngài Tông-khách-ba cũng là vị Tổ có ảnh hưởng sâu sắc với Tập đoàn/ Tăng đoàn Phúc Trí chúng tôi với giáo nghĩa trong *Bộ Quảng Luận* – bộ luận kim chỉ nam để Tăng Ni Cư sĩ Phúc Trí Đài Loan hành trì qua bốn bước chính: (1) Căn bản trước khi vào đạo: sự thù thắng của bậc đạo sư, giáo pháp, nương tựa vào thiện tri thức và thiết lập nền tảng tổng quát của đạo. (2) Tiểu thừa chung: quy y và nhân quả nghiệp báo, con đường tu tập để có được đời sống tốt đẹp trong tương lai. (3) Trung thừa chung: tứ diệu đế và thập nhị nhân duyên, nhắm hướng đến con đường giải thoát. (4) Thượng thừa: bồ đề tâm, lục độ ba la mật và tứ nhiếp pháp để độ hóa chúng sinh, tiến đến thành tựu Bồ-đề vô thượng.

Tác phẩm của Ngài Drupa Rinpoche (Lobsang Yeshi) đã chỉ ra, có bốn loại Bát-nhã Ba-la-mật (Perfection of Wisdom): (1) Tự tánh bát-nhã - chính là *tánh Không*; (2) Giáo thuyết bát-nhã - tức là *các kinh điển giảng giải về tính không*; (3) Đạo bát-nhã - trí tuệ *quán chiếu tánh Không* trên lộ trình tu tập; (4) Quả bát-nhã - trí tuệ viên mãn nơi một vị Phật đã hoàn toàn giác ngộ. Riêng giáo thuyết Bát-nhã (tức các bản kinh) được phân thành nhiều cấp độ: (1) Quảng bản (bản rộng) (Bhum) - gồm 100.000 bài tụng; (2) Trung bản (Nyi Tri) - gồm 25.000 bài tụng; (3) Bản thiểu (bản ngắn) (Gye Tongpa) - gồm 8.000 bài tụng; (4) Bản tinh yếu - chính là *Bát-nhã Tâm Kinh*; phần tinh tuý - giống như bơ được chưng từ sữa - trong toàn bộ giáo pháp của Đức Phật, *Bát-nhã Tâm Kinh* là tinh yếu được cô đọng từ kho tàng mênh mông của giáo lý *Bát-nhã ba-la-mật*.

Tôi rất tâm đắc với tác phẩm của Ngài Drupa Rinpoche (Lobsang Yeshi) đã đưa ra quan điểm của phái Trung Quán Cụ Duyên (Prāsaṅgika), hành giả thuộc Thanh văn (śrāvaka) hay Độc giác (pratyekabuddha) hoặc đang hành trì con đường Đại thừa, nếu chấp ngã chấp pháp rất khó liễu ngộ Tính Không tự tính. Phần trí tuệ của đạo lộ chính là sự chứng ngộ Tính Không; chủ trương các pháp chỉ là những phóng chiếu của tâm thức; mọi hiện tượng đều không tồn tại một cách độc lập, không có thực thể cố định; chúng chỉ hiện hữu tùy thuộc vào duyên khởi. Từ đó, hành giả có thể ứng hiện thể - tướng - dụng vào mọi hoàn cảnh của tục đế, hành Bồ-tát hạnh đem lại an lạc và hạnh phúc cho chúng sanh trên tinh thần "tự độ độ tha" nhờ nhận thức sâu sắc "ngã không pháp không". Tôi chân thành tán thán và giới thiệu độc giả Quốc tế, cùng lan tỏa giáo Pháp, minh triết của Phật giáo; cùng nhau xây dựng và kiến tạo xã hội văn minh, tiến bộ, hòa bình, bền vững theo tiêu chí của Vesak Liên Hợp Quốc 2025 tạo Việt Nam đã đưa ra.

Đài Loan, tháng 8/2025

Phó giáo sư – Tiến sĩ Quách Cơ Thụy Frank, J.R. GUO

Giám đốc Điều hành quỹ Văn hóa & Giáo dục Phúc Trí – Đài Loan

Chủ tịch Tổ chức bảo tồn Nho giáo Toàn cầu

Nguyên giáo sư, giảng viên Đại học Y tế Quốc gia Cao Hùng

Bát-nhã Tâm Kinh là một bản kinh rất nổi tiếng. Tôi tin rằng hầu hết các truyền thống Phật giáo đều có bản kinh này được dịch sang ngôn ngữ của riêng mình và có phiên bản phù hợp với truyền thống đó. Đối với người Tây Tạng, *Bát-nhã Tâm Kinh* là một trong những bản kinh được trì tụng hằng ngày phổ biến nhất. Kinh thường được tụng trước mỗi buổi giảng pháp, đặc biệt là những buổi do Thánh Đức Đạt-lai Lạt-ma chủ trì.

Mặc dù rất phổ biến và hiện diện khắp nơi, *Bát-nhã Tâm Kinh* vẫn là một bản kinh hết sức thâm sâu và khó lãnh hội. Cốt lõi của kinh là giáo lý về tánh Không. *Bát-nhã Tâm Kinh*, cũng như bất kỳ pháp nào liên quan đến khái niệm tánh Không, thường được gọi là ma sam joe mi, nghĩa là "bất khả tư nghì" - vượt ngoài ngôn ngữ thông thường, vượt khỏi tư duy khái niệm thông tục. Ngay cả những bậc đã chứng ngộ sâu xa về tánh Không cũng thấy khó diễn bày. Bởi vậy, tự nhiên là tôi cũng gặp khó khăn trong việc giải thích điều này.

Bát-nhã Tâm Kinh có thể được giảng dạy ở nhiều tầng mức khác nhau. Các bậc đạo sư có thể dành nhiều ngày để khai triển các chiều kích triết lý của kinh. Trong *LAMRIM CHENMO* (Đại Luận Tu Tuấn), chỉ riêng phần nói về "đối tượng bị phủ định" đã kéo dài từ 30 đến 60 trang. Nhiều bậc học giả trong quá khứ đã hiểu sai giáo pháp của Đức Phật về tánh Không. Chính vì thế, những tác phẩm như *LAMRIM CHENMO* nhấn mạnh tầm quan trọng của việc nhận thức chính xác điều gì là đối tượng bị phủ định, khi ta nói rằng một pháp là "không".

Tôi không thể đi sâu vào đề tài này đến mức ấy. Tôi không có đủ tuệ giác hay năng lực để trình bày một cách thật chi tiết. Vì thế, thật đáng tiếc cho quý vị - quý vị lại gặp tôi để giúp hiểu phần nào về bản kinh này. Tuy nhiên, tôi vẫn sẽ cố gắng lần lượt đi qua từng câu trong kinh và đưa ra một vài lời giải thích. Trong tiếng Tây Tạng, cách trình bày này gọi là *tsig-'drel*, tức là giải thích từng từ hoặc từng cụm từ.

Bát-nhã Tâm Kinh từ lâu đã được dịch sang tiếng Anh, và khi đọc lần đầu, kinh có thể có vẻ đơn giản một cách dễ gây ngộ nhận. Tuy nhiên, nếu không có chút hiểu biết nào về tánh Không, người đọc sẽ khó mà lĩnh hội được ý nghĩa của kinh. Những cụm như "không mắt, không tai, không mũi..." có thể khiến ta hoang mang. Nhưng một khi ta nắm được khái niệm tánh Không, mọi điều dường như bắt đầu sáng tỏ. Đó chính là mục tiêu của chúng ta ở đây - cùng cố gắng hiểu được rốt ráo điều mà bản kinh sâu xa này đang chỉ bày.

TÂM KINH LÀ GÌ

***Bát-nhã Tâm Kinh* là gì?**

Kinh này được gọi là *Tinh yếu của Kinh Bát-nhã Ba-la-mật-đa*. Đức Phật đã tuyên thuyết vô lượng giáo pháp - theo truyền thống được tóm lược thành tám vạn bốn nghìn pháp tạng - và những giáo pháp ấy được giảng dạy theo từng giai đoạn, thường được phân loại thành Ba lần Chuyển bánh xe Chánh Pháp.

- *Lần Chuyển bánh xe Chánh Pháp thứ nhất* tập trung vào giáo lý *Tứ Diệu Đế.*
- *Lần Chuyển thứ hai* trình bày giáo pháp về *Bát-nhã Ba-la-mật-đa* (tánh Không).
- *Lần Chuyển thứ ba* làm rõ những lời dạy của Đức Phật về tánh Không.

Bát-nhã Tâm Kinh thuộc về hệ thống giáo pháp về tánh Không, được tuyên thuyết trong *Lần Chuyển bánh xe Chánh Pháp thứ hai.*

Sau khi chứng đắc Vô thượng Bồ-đề, Đức Phật ban đầu giữ im lặng. Ngài cảm thấy những điều đã liễu ngộ là quá triệt để, quá mang tính cách mạng, đến nỗi con người khó có thể lĩnh hội. Những điều ấy hoàn toàn trái ngược với tất cả những gì con người vốn tin là thực tại. Cuối cùng, sau khi được Thiên Chủ Đế Thích (Śakra) khẩn thỉnh, Đức Phật bắt đầu chuyển pháp luân. Bài pháp đầu tiên của Ngài là Tứ Diệu Đế, được tuyên thuyết tại Lộc Uyển (*Sarnath*).

Tất cả chúng ta đều khao khát hạnh phúc và tìm cách tránh né khổ đau. Để đạt được điều đó, Đức Phật dạy rằng trước hết chúng ta phải nhận diện nỗi khổ (Đệ nhất Diệu Đế). Phần lớn mọi người chỉ hiểu khổ là đau đớn về thân thể hoặc những cảm thọ khó chịu rõ rệt, nhưng Đức Phật đã chỉ ra ba loại khổ:

1. **Khổ khổ** - nỗi khổ do chính cảm thọ khổ gây ra (như đau đớn thân xác rõ rệt);

2. **Hoại khổ** - nỗi khổ do biến đổi, khi lạc biến thành khổ vì vô thường;

3. **Hành khổ** - nỗi khổ thâm sâu, lan tỏa trong toàn thể sự hiện hữu do duyên sinh điều kiện.

Để diệt trừ khổ đau, chúng ta cần hiểu rõ nguyên nhân của khổ - chính là các vọng tưởng và phiền não - đó là Đệ nhị Diệu Đế (Tập đế). Khi những nguyên nhân ấy được nhổ tận gốc, khổ đau sẽ tự nhiên chấm dứt - đó là Đệ tam Diệu Đế, tức Diệt đế. Để đạt được sự chấm dứt khổ đau này, chúng ta cần hành trì con đường tu tập - những phương pháp nhằm đoạn trừ vọng tưởng và phiền não - đó là *Đệ tứ Diệu Đế*, tức *Đạo đế*.

Con đường tối hậu để đoạn trừ tận gốc khổ đau là trí tuệ quán chiếu tánh Không. Để khai triển rõ hơn về con đường này, Đức Phật đã tuyên thuyết thêm nhiều giáo pháp, trong đó có giáo lý *Duyên khởi* - tức là mọi pháp (bao gồm cả khổ đau và hạnh phúc) đều sinh khởi từ nhân duyên, với căn nhân chính yếu là *vô minh* - tức là sự không liễu tri về tánh Không của các pháp.

Trong tác phẩm *Trung Quán Luận* của Bồ Tát Long Thọ (*Nāgārjuna*), Ngài viết:

"Bị vô minh che lấp, vì mục đích tái sinh, chúng ta tạo ra ba loại nghiệp - chính các nghiệp này cấu thành sự hiện hữu và thúc đẩy chúng ta trôi lăn trong vòng luân hồi (sinh tử)."

Chính những hành vi (nghiệp) ấy dẫn chúng sinh tái sinh vào ba cõi: **Dục giới** (bao gồm cõi người và các cõi thấp hơn), **Sắc giới** và **Vô sắc giới**. Ngay cả những tầng thiền định cao trong **Vô sắc giới**, nếu không được khởi phát từ tâm nguyện cầu giải thoát khỏi vòng sinh tử luân hồi, vẫn tiếp tục ràng buộc chúng sinh trong **luân hồi**.

Tổ Tông-khách-ba (*Tsongkhapa*), trong *LUẬN BA YẾU TỐ CHÍNH CỦA ĐẠO LỘ*, đã viết:

"Nếu không có trí tuệ chứng ngộ thực tại tối hậu, thì dù có phát khởi tâm xả ly và Bồ-đề tâm, cũng không thể đoạn trừ tận gốc luân hồi sinh tử."

Nói cách khác, **nếu không có tuệ giác quán chiếu tánh Không**, thì không có con đường nào có thể đoạn trừ khổ đau tận gốc. Chính Đức Phật (khi còn là Thái tử Tất-đạt-đa) cũng đã trải qua một quá trình lâu dài để chứng ngộ điều này.

Khi còn sống trong cung điện, Thái tử Tất-đạt-đa đã hành thiền và đạt được một mức độ thiền định nhất định. Không thỏa mãn với mức chứng ấy, Ngài đã từ bỏ đời sống vương giả để xuất gia. Sau đó, Ngài tìm đến các vị đạo sư Ấn Độ danh tiếng thời bấy giờ và tiếp tục hành thiền theo chỉ dẫn của họ.

Khi đạt đến **tầng định cao nhất trong luân hồi** - được gọi là *hữu đảnh định* (bhava-agra-samāpatti) - Thái tử Tất-đạt-đa đến gặp vị thầy của mình và hỏi: "Liệu còn điều gì vượt lên trên cảnh giới này không?" Vị thầy đáp rằng trạng thái này chính là Niết-bàn, và không còn gì cần được học thêm nữa.Tuy nhiên, Tất-đạt-đa không tin rằng trạng thái ấy là sự giải thoát chân thật, nên Ngài tiếp tục hành trình tìm cầu. Với Ngài, những tầng thiền định đó không chạm đến tận gốc rễ của khổ; chúng chỉ làm suy giảm các đối tượng của ái (tham luyến), nhưng không đoạn tận được chấp thủ từ căn bản.

Chúng sinh thuộc **Dục giới** (bao gồm cõi người) đuổi theo các dục lạc cảm quan. Chúng sinh **Sắc giới** đã vượt qua dục ái thô thiển, thay vào đó tìm cầu lạc thọ phát sinh từ thiền định, rốt ráo hướng đến xả thọ (cảm giác trung tính). Chúng sinh thuộc **Vô sắc giới** lìa bỏ toàn bộ sắc pháp, chỉ còn an trụ nơi tâm, rồi tuần tự tiến vào các tầng thiền định vi tế: **hư không vô biên xứ**, **thức vô biên xứ**, **vô sở hữu xứ**, và sau cùng là **phi tưởng phi phi tưởng xứ**.

Nhiều tông phái phi Phật giáo tại Ấn Độ xem các tầng thiền định này là cứu cánh tối hậu - tức giải thoát. Tuy nhiên, theo quan điểm của Phật giáo, chừng nào các tầng định ấy **không được phối hợp với trí tuệ quán chiếu tánh Không**, thì hành giả vẫn bị vô minh chi phối, vẫn còn trầm luân trong **l**uân hồi sinh tử, và vì thế vẫn phải chịu khổ.

Cuối cùng, Thái tử Tất-đạt-đa liễu ngộ rằng có **hai loại chấp thủ: chấp ngã** (chấp vào một tự ngã hiện hữu thật) và **chấp pháp** (chấp các pháp là có tự tính hiện thực). Hai loại chấp này chính là **căn nguyên của ái** (tham luyến), và do đó là **nguồn gốc của khổ đau**.

Trong các tình huống xã hội, chẳng hạn như tranh cãi trong gia đình, nếu quán chiếu sâu sắc, ta sẽ nhận thấy **gốc rễ của xung đột là cảm giác chấp thủ mãnh liệt vào cái "tôi".** Ta bảo vệ cái "tôi" ấy, khởi tâm luyến ái đối với những ai ủng hộ nó, và sân hận với những ai đe dọa đến nó. Chính cái "tôi" giả lập và kiên cố ấy là cốt lõi của mọi khổ đau.

Giáo lý về **tánh Không** nhằm quán chiếu bản chất chân thật của cái "tôi" vốn dường như tuyệt đối. Vì thế, việc **thấu hiểu tánh Không-rốt ráo nhận ra rằng cái "tôi" ấy không hề hiện hữu một cách tự tính**-là điều hết sức trọng yếu. Thật vậy, đây có thể trở thành **pháp dược nhiệm mầu** giúp chuyển hoá mọi khổ lụy của chúng ta.

Một vị đại học giả từng kể lại câu chuyện sau:

Có một người cha có ba người con trai. Khi còn khoẻ mạnh, ông đã chia tài sản cho cả ba. Hai người con lớn rời khỏi nhà, chỉ còn người con út ở lại. Người con út được giao phó việc chăm sóc cha mình. Hai người con lớn thì thờ ơ, không hề giúp đỡ. Một người bạn của người cha trông thấy cảnh ấy, liền nghĩ ra một kế hoạch.

Người ấy mang đến một chiếc hộp lớn và nặng, rồi nói với người cha: "Đây là vật mà ông đã dặn tôi trao lại khi ông lâm vào cảnh khốn khó." Chiếc hộp được khóa kín, còn chìa khóa thì đeo ngay trên cổ của người cha.

Người con út, tưởng rằng trong hộp có châu báu, bỗng trở nên hết sức tử tế, chăm sóc ân cần và đầy thương kính. Hai người anh thấy sự thay đổi ấy, biết đến chiếc hộp, cũng bắt đầu tỏ ra quan tâm đến người cha, mong có phần thừa hưởng. Cuối cùng, người cha qua đời. Họ mở hộp ra - chỉ thấy toàn những hòn đá. Tất cả hành động của họ đều dựa trên một giả định sai lầm.

Câu chuyện này phản ánh mối tương quan giữa chúng ta và cảm nhận sai lầm về "ngã". Chúng ta đã kiến lập một ý niệm tinh vi về một cái "ngã" kiên cố, có thật. Nhưng thực chất, **không hề có một cái "ngã" hiện hữu tự tính.** Chỉ có một **khái niệm về "ngã"** được gán đặt lên **ngũ uẩn** (sắc và tâm) mà thôi. Thế mà chúng ta lại khổ đau và lao nhọc vì cái "ngã" hư vọng ấy.

Đây chính là **tinh yếu của *Bát-nhã Tâm Kinh*** - một phần trong *Lần Chuyển Pháp Luân thứ hai*. *Tâm Kinh* chưng cất tinh túy của toàn bộ giáo pháp *Bát-nhã ba-la-mật* về **tính không**.

Đây chính là ***tinh yếu của Bát-nhã Tâm Kinh*** - một phần thuộc *Lần Chuyển Pháp Luân* thứ hai. *Bát-nhã Tâm Kinh* cô đọng tinh túy của toàn bộ giáo pháp Bát-nhã Ba-la-mật về tánh Không.

Có **bốn loại Bát-nhã Ba-la-mật (Perfection of Wisdom)**:

1. **Tự tánh bát-nhã** - chính là *tánh Không*;
2. **Giáo thuyết bát-nhã** - tức là *các kinh điển giảng giải về tính không*;
3. **Đạo bát-nhã** - trí tuệ *quán chiếu tánh Không* trên lộ trình tu tập;
4. **Quả bát-nhã** - trí tuệ viên mãn nơi một vị Phật đã hoàn toàn giác ngộ.

Riêng **giáo thuyết Bát-nhã** (tức các bản kinh) được phân thành nhiều cấp độ:

- **Quảng bản (bản rộng) (Bhum)** - gồm **100.000 bài tụng**;
- **Trung bản (Nyi Tri)** - gồm **25.000 bài tụng**;
- **Bản thiểu (bản ngắn) (Gye Tongpa)** - gồm **8.000 bài tụng**;
- **Bản tinh yếu** - chính là *Bát-nhã Tâm Kinh*.

Vào những ngày đặc biệt hoặc trong các nghi lễ, chư Tăng tụng đọc những bản kinh này, đặc biệt là bản 8.000 bài tụng (*Gye Tongpa*). Việc tụng các bản quảng có thể kéo dài nhiều ngày. Còn Bát-nhã Tâm Kinh thì được cô đọng lại như bơ được chưng ra từ sữa - chính là tinh tuý thanh khiết nhất của toàn bộ giáo pháp.

Khi tôi còn nhỏ, cha tôi thường tự tay làm bơ. Trước tiên, ông lên men sữa thành sữa đông, rồi cho vào một ống gỗ có gắn cánh khuấy. Ông quấn quanh người một tấm vải - không hẳn là tạp dề, mà giống như một mảnh vải thô buộc ngang thân - rồi bắt đầu khuấy bằng cách đẩy và kéo cánh khuấy gỗ lên xuống bên trong ống. Cách ông khuấy có một tiết tấu đều đặn; cứ sau vài trăm lượt khuấy, ông lại châm thêm một ít nước ấm. Không hiểu sao, ông luôn biết chính xác khi nào bơ đã kết thành. Khoảnh khắc ấy luôn khiến tôi không khỏi kinh ngạc

Tại sao tôi kể câu chuyện này? Vì *Bát-nhã Tâm Kinh* chính là **phần tinh tuý** - giống như **bơ** được chưng từ sữa - trong toàn bộ giáo pháp của Đức Phật. Cũng như bơ là kết quả của quá trình khuấy liên tục sữa và kem, *Bát-nhã Tâm Kinh* là tinh yếu được cô đọng từ kho tàng mênh mông của giáo lý *Bát-nhã ba-la-mật*. Và đó chính là điều mà chúng ta sẽ cùng nhau nỗ lực tìm hiểu ở đây.

Tại Tây Tạng, **kinh điển thường được in theo phương pháp truyền thống bằng bản khắc gỗ.** Mỗi chữ đều được khắc tay lên các bản gỗ. Có thể thấy trong nhiều bức ảnh ghi lại cảnh hai người đàn ông đang in kinh văn: đầu tiên, họ cẩn thận cắt giấy theo kích cỡ chuẩn, sau đó thoa mực lên bản khắc, đặt giấy lên trên, rồi dùng miếng gạt để ép mực in lên giấy. Đó là một quá trình tỉ mỉ, đòi hỏi nhiều công phu - nhưng chính bằng cách ấy mà kinh sách được hình thành.

Liên quan đến cách thức bảo tồn **kinh điển**, cần biết rằng Đức Phật đã tuyên thuyết giáo pháp tại nhiều nơi, nhưng **trong suốt thời gian tại thế, không có lời dạy nào được ghi chép thành văn bản.** Tất cả đều được truyền thừa bằng **khẩu truyền**. Sau khi Đức Phật nhập Niết-bàn, các **đại hội kết tập kinh điển** được tổ chức, trong đó các vị đệ tử - những bậc đã **ghi nhớ lời dạy của Ngài** - cùng nhau tụng đọc lại các pháp thoại, và từ đó mới được chép lại thành văn. Đây đều là những hành giả có **công phu**

thiền định thâm sâu và **trí nhớ phi thường**, nhờ đó có thể ghi nhớ lời Phật dạy với **sự minh bạch và chính xác cao độ**.

Thậm chí có một truyền thuyết kể rằng, sau khi Đức Phật nhập diệt, các loài hữu tình - gồm **nhân loại, chư thiên, a-tu-la và long vương** - đã tụ hội để bàn luận xem ai sẽ là vị **giữ gìn những giáo pháp thâm diệu** này. Vì không thể đi đến đồng thuận, các bản kinh được cho là đã bị **phân tán khắp mọi phương.**

Một truyền thuyết cho rằng **các bộ kinh Bát-nhã ba-la-mật** đã được **long tộc (Nāga)** gìn giữ trong cõi long tộc. Về sau, Bồ-tát **Long Thọ (Nāgārjuna)** đã đến **cõi long tộc** và thỉnh các bản kinh ấy. Điều thú vị là, người ta truyền rằng **long tộc không trao trả toàn bộ các phẩm kinh**, mà **giữ lại một số chương** như một hình thức bảo chứng nhằm khuyến khích Long Thọ quay lại. Do vậy, **trong một số bản kinh Bát-nhã ba-la-mật**, có **những phẩm bị khuyết lạc**.

BỐI CẢNH TRIẾT HỌC

Trước khi đi sâu vào *Bát-nhã Tâm Kinh*, chúng ta cần có sự hiểu biết căn bản về bốn tông phái tư tưởng chính trong Phật giáo và quan điểm của họ về vô ngã.

Quan điểm về vô ngã: Bốn tông phái chính

- **Tông Hữu bộ (Vaibhāṣika)** - Vô ngã của ngã thể
- **Tông Kinh lượng bộ (Sautrāntika)** - Vô ngã của ngã thể
- **Tông Duy thức (Cittamātra)** - Vô ngã của ngã thể và vô ngã của chư pháp
- **Tông Trung quán (Mādhyamika)** - Vô ngã của ngã thể và vô ngã của chư pháp

- **Tông Tự lập Trung quán (Svātantrika)** - Chấp nhận tính hiện hữu nội tại ở cấp độ tối hậu

- **Tông Y tha khởi Trung quán (Prāsaṅgika)** - Bác bỏ hoàn toàn tính hiện hữu nội tại ở cấp độ tối hậu

Quan điểm Phật giáo và phi Phật giáo về ngã

Các **truyền thống phi Phật giáo** thường khẳng định rằng "ngã" là **thường hằng, đơn nhất và độc lập** - tức một ngã thể **tồn tại độc lập ngoài thân và tâm** (ngũ uẩn). Quan niệm này hàm ý rằng ngã không bị chi phối bởi các yếu tố vật chất hay tâm lý cấu thành con người.

Ngược lại, **Phật giáo** khẳng định rằng **không có một "ngã" nào tồn tại độc lập với các uẩn**. "Ngã" sinh khởi một cách tùy thuộc. Nói cách khác, "ngã" nương vào ngũ uẩn mà hiện khởi - **chỉ là một giả danh quy ước** do tâm phân biệt gán đặt.

Trong **bốn tông phái tư tưởng Phật giáo**, hai tông đầu tiên là:

- **Hữu bộ (Vaibhāṣika)**
- **Kinh lượng bộ (Sautrāntika)**

Cả hai đều nhấn mạnh vào **giáo lý vô ngã của ngã thể** (phủ định ngã thể trong cá nhân). Hai tông phái này cho rằng chỉ cần **chứng ngộ được vô ngã của ngã thể là đủ để đạt đến Niết-bàn hoặc giải thoát**. Họ **không luận giải về vô ngã của chư pháp.**

Hai tông còn lại là Duy thức tông (Cittamātra - Duy tâm tông) và Trung quán tông (Mādhyamika - Trung đạo tông), chủ trương cả **vô ngã của ngã thể** và **vô ngã của chư pháp**. Mục tiêu của hai tông này vượt lên trên giải thoát cá nhân; **họ nhắm đến giác ngộ viên mãn (Phật quả)**. Họ luận về **hai tầng chướng ngại cần đoạn trừ để thành tựu giác ngộ viên mãn:**

1. **Phiền não chướng (kleśa-āvaraṇa)**: các **phiền não như tham, sân, si** - chướng ngại cho sự giải thoát.
2. **Sở tri chướng (jñeya-āvaraṇa)**: tức là các **chướng ngại nhận thức, vọng tưởng, tà kiến**, chướng ngại cho trí tuệ **toàn giác (nhất thiết trí)**.

Để **đoạn trừ sở tri chướng**, hành giả cần chứng ngộ không chỉ **vô ngã của ngã thể**, mà còn cả **vô ngã của chư pháp** - tức là thấy rõ **tất cả hiện tượng đều không có tự tính**, chỉ tồn tại do **duyên khởi và quy ước**.

Vô ngã và Duyên khởi

Trong **bốn tông phái Phật giáo**, có những **sai biệt vi tế** trong cách họ quan niệm về vô ngã. Chẳng hạn, **Trung quán Cụ duyên (Prāsa⊠gika Madhyamika)** - thường được xem là **tông phái triết học tối thượng** - khẳng định rằng **không pháp nào hiện hữu từ tự thân.**

Ngược lại, **ba tông phái còn lại** cho rằng cần **phải có một thực thể hiện hữu nội tại** làm nền tảng cho sự gán danh. Họ thường nêu một ví dụ:

“Để được gọi là bác sĩ, một người phải học y khoa và đạt đủ điều kiện chuyên môn. Chỉ khi đó, danh xưng ‘bác sĩ’ mới được xem là đúng đắn.”

Theo lập luận của họ, việc đơn thuần **gán danh bằng tâm thức là chưa đủ**; cần phải có một **nền tảng hiện hữu từ phía tự thân** để làm căn cứ cho danh xưng ấy.

Chính ở điểm này mà quan kiến của phái **Prāsaṅgika** trở nên độc đáo: họ chủ trương rằng **ngay cả nền tảng để thiết lập danh xưng cũng không hiện hữu một cách tự tính**. Mọi pháp - bao gồm cả nền tảng của sự quy ước danh xưng - **đều rỗng không về tự tính**. Những gì chúng ta gọi là “bác sĩ” hay “con người” **chỉ là những danh xưng do tâm thức gán đặt**, dựa trên sự kết hợp của các bộ phận và chức năng - **không có một tự thể nội tại nào ẩn sau những danh xưng ấy.**

Điều này trở nên **đặc biệt quan trọng khi quán chiếu Bát-nhã Tâm Kinh**. Kinh văn có đoạn:

“Không có mắt, không có tai, không có mũi… không có sắc, không có thanh, không có hương…”

Đối với người chưa quen với giáo lý về tính không, những lời ấy dường như vô nghĩa. Nhưng khi có tuệ giác về **tính không** và **duyên khởi** - tức là thấy rõ rằng các pháp sinh khởi trong sự nương tựa vào các yếu tố như **nhân, duyên, các bộ phận cấu thành và sự gán đặt của tâm thức** - thì **ý nghĩa sâu xa** của những câu kinh ấy mới hiển lộ.

Kinh văn **không phủ nhận sự hiện hữu quy ước của các pháp**, mà **phủ định sự hiện hữu tự tính hay sự tồn tại một cách độc lập** của chúng. Trong các tông phái Phật giáo cấp thấp hơn, chư vị ấy vẫn nỗ lực **xác định "ngã" nằm ở đâu**. Có vị cho rằng **sáu thức (lục thức)** chính là ngã, và tuyên bố:

"Chính đó là ngã."

Tông Duy thức (Cittamātra) bác bỏ quan điểm ấy bằng lập luận rằng **sáu thức không thể là ngã**, mà thay vào đó, họ chỉ định một **thức đặc biệt** gọi là **tàng thức (ālayavijñāna)** - kho chứa tất cả các **chủng tử nghiệp** - làm ngã. Những quan điểm này phát sinh từ **niềm tin rằng phải có một thực thể nào đó hiện hữu từ phía tự thân**. Nếu chấp vào quan kiến như vậy, thì **ắt phải xác định được một pháp thể tồn tại một cách độc lập và thật có - như là ngã, hoặc đối tượng.**

Một số quan điểm khác có thể nhìn vào một vật như điện thoại di động và cho rằng: "Điện thoại là sự kết hợp của các bộ phận cấu thành." Khi áp dụng lối tư duy này vào cái ngã, họ có thể chỉ vào **thức** và cho rằng đó là ngã. Nhưng quan điểm của **phái Trung Quán Prāsaṅgika** thì khác biệt. Họ y cứ theo lời dạy của Đức Phật: "Không có thực thể nào thật sự hiện hữu." Trên nền tảng đó, họ **khẳng định tính vô ngã của các pháp.**

Theo quan điểm của **phái Trung Quán Cụ Duyên (Prāsaṅgika)**, dù là **hành giả thuộc Tiểu thừa** - tức bậc **Thanh văn (śrāvaka)** hay **Độc giác (pratyekabuddha)** - hoặc đang **hành trì con đường Đại thừa**, thì

đều không thể đạt đến giải thoát nếu chưa chứng ngộ tính không của sự hiện hữu tự tính.

Phần trí tuệ của đạo lộ **chính là sự chứng ngộ tính không**. Theo quan điểm của **phái Trung Quán Cụ Duyên (Prāsaṅgika)**, các cách hiểu về **vô ngã** được trình bày bởi các tông phái khác **còn quá thô phù**. Những quan kiến ấy **không đủ sâu để tận diệt tận gốc vô minh**. Vì vậy, phái này chủ trương rằng **các pháp không hiện hữu từ phía tự thân; chúng chỉ là những phóng chiếu của tâm thức lên một nền tảng** (Nói cách khác, mọi hiện tượng - dù là ngã hay pháp - **đều không tồn tại một cách độc lập, khách quan, có thực thể cố định**. Chúng **chỉ hiện hữu như những khái niệm được tâm thức gán đặt**, tùy thuộc vào duyên khởi và tương quan.).

Tính không (*śūnyatā*)

Đối tượng cần phủ định: Sự hiện hữu tự tính / Bản chất nội tại / Cái ngã tuyệt đối / Thực tại khách quan / Hiện hữu từ phía tự thân
Trung đạo: Vượt khỏi **hai cực đoan: Chấp thường** và **Chấp đoạn**
Chấp thường *(Absolutism):*
Nếu một pháp hiện hữu, thì nó **phải hiện hữu một cách tự tính.**
Chấp đoạn *(Nihilism):*
Nếu phủ nhận sự hiện hữu tự tính, thì suy ra rằng **không có gì hiện hữu cả.**
Cần phân biệt rõ ràng giữa:
*** Hiện hữu quy ước (merely existent) ↔ Hiện hữu tự tính (inherently existent)**
*** Không hiện hữu (nonexistent) ↔ Không hiện hữu tự tính (non inherently existent)**

Hãy xét một ví dụ kinh điển thường được dùng như một phép thí dụ: hãy tưởng tượng bạn thấy một sợi dây cuộn trong bóng tối. Nhìn thoáng qua, nó có vẻ như là một con rắn. Bạn khởi tâm sợ hãi - tim đập nhanh. Nhưng khi quan sát kỹ hơn, bạn nhận ra đó chỉ là một sợi dây. Nỗi sợ ấy, tuy dựa trên một nhận thức sai lầm, nhưng cảm thọ ấy lại hoàn toàn có thật. Ảo ảnh như mộng về con rắn ấy đã gây ra phản ứng cảm thọ chân thật. Tương tự, trong giấc mơ, ta có thể kinh hoàng vì một con quái vật. Nỗi sợ hãi, sự vã mồ hôi, tim đập nhanh - tất cả đều là những phản ứng có thật trước một hoàn cảnh không thật. Chính tâm thức đã phóng chiếu các hình tướng.

Nếu các pháp thực sự hiện hữu từ phía tự thân, thì những huyễn tướng như vậy đã không thể khởi hiện. Theo quan điểm của phái Trung Quán Cụ Duyên (Prāsaṅgika), các pháp giống như huyễn, như mộng. Những gì chúng ta thấy chỉ là sự phóng chiếu - không phải là sự phản ánh của một tự tính cố hữu.

Sự phóng chiếu và tri nhận

Hãy hình dung một chiếc **máy chiếu phim**. **Màn hình** vốn hoàn toàn trống rỗng, như một ***tabula rasa***. Khi cuộn phim bắt đầu chạy, những **hình ảnh sinh động, hấp dẫn hiện lên**. Nhưng kỳ thực, **đó chỉ là những hình ảnh được phóng chiếu** - chúng không có thực thể nơi chính màn hình. Cũng vậy, **tâm thức phóng chiếu các hình tướng lên con người, sự vật và hoàn cảnh**, rồi **chúng ta chấp thủ chúng như thể đó là thực tại.**

Vì thế, theo quan điểm của **phái Trung Quán Cụ Duyên (Prāsaṅgika Madhyamaka), các pháp chỉ tồn tại thông qua sự gán danh khái niệm (*conceptual designation*) trên một nền tảng**. Nói cách khác, **sự hiện hữu của các pháp không đến từ phía tự thân**, mà **chỉ là sự tồn tại trong danh ngôn - do tâm thức phân biệt đặt tên lên một tập hợp các yếu tố duyên khởi.**

Ứng dụng vào đời sống thực tiễn

Có người từng chia sẻ một trải nghiệm nơi công sở. Người quản lý - vốn không có thiện cảm với cô - đã **quở trách cô một cách gay gắt.** Ngay trong khoảnh khắc ấy, cô chợt khởi lên một tuệ giác: "Sự khó chịu này - những gì tôi đang nghe và thấy - **chỉ là sự phóng chiếu của tâm thức tôi**. Vị sếp ấy giống như **một màn ảnh trắng**, và chính **những chủng tử nghiệp tiêu cực trong quá khứ** đã khiến tôi **phóng chiếu một cách tiêu cực lên màn ảnh đó** (tức là vị sếp)." Khi suy nghĩ như vậy, **cơn giận trong cô lập tức lắng xuống,** sự phiền não và khổ thọ cũng theo đó chấm dứt. Thay vào đó là một sự **hiểu biết mới và một tâm nguyện muốn làm dịu tình huống.** Từ nơi trực cảm, cô thốt lên: "Có điều gì tôi có thể giúp được không?" Vị sếp hoàn toàn bất ngờ. **Sự chuyển hóa cảm xúc phát khởi từ sự thấu triệt bản chất của các phóng chiếu tâm thức.**

Khi nghe những lời khó chịu, chúng ta thường có khuynh hướng **khởi tâm sân hận** và **phản ứng tiêu cực**. Chẳng hạn, khi bị cấp trên phê bình rằng: "Công việc này tệ quá!", ta thường **vướng mắc vào chữ "tệ"**. Tuy nhiên, nếu **vận dụng tuệ giác về tính không** và **quán chiếu cụm từ "công việc tệ"**, ta sẽ thấy rằng: mặc dù nó **có vẻ như hiện hữu một cách chắc thật từ phía đối tượng**, nhưng **kỳ thực, không có gì "tệ" một cách tự tính cả.** Đó **chỉ là một danh xưng được gán đặt** cho một phương diện nào đó của công việc, dựa trên **quan điểm của cấp trên** và **các yếu tố hoàn cảnh xung quanh**. Không có gì "tệ" một cách **khách quan hay độc lập**, ngoài **nhận thức của người phê bình** và **những điều kiện tương quan**. Nếu công việc ấy thực sự "tệ" một cách tự tính, thì **bất kỳ ai** - dù là đồng nghiệp, một cấp trên khác, hay trong những điều kiện khác - cũng tất phải thấy nó là "tệ". Nhưng thực tế, **một người khác có thể xem đó là một công việc xuất sắc.**

Một ví dụ khác minh họa rõ ràng **tính phi tự tính của khái niệm "tốt" hay "xấu"** là việc **tăng cân.** Tôi được biết rằng trong **văn hóa phương**

Tây, việc tăng cân thường mang **hàm ý tiêu cực**, và việc nhận xét điều đó bị xem là **bất lịch sự**. Ngược lại, trong **văn hóa Tây Tạng**, việc nói ai đó tăng cân lại được xem như một **lời khen**. Người Tây Tạng lớn tuổi thường nhận xét về cân nặng của người khác, **thể hiện sự lo lắng chân thành** nếu ai đó sụt cân, và **hoan hỷ** khi thấy một người nào đó có vẻ tăng cân. Vì vậy, trong cộng đồng Tây Tạng, người ta thường có phản ứng tích cực trước những nhận xét như vậy - họ cảm thấy **hoan hỷ** khi được nói rằng mình có vẻ tăng cân, và sẽ **lo lắng** nếu được bảo rằng mình trở nên gầy hơn. Điều này **hoàn toàn trái ngược với phản ứng thường thấy ở nhiều người lớn lên trong văn hóa phương Tây**. Đối với người Tây Tạng lớn tuổi, việc **tăng cân được xem là điều tốt,** còn **sụt cân là điều không tốt**; ngược lại, với nhiều người phương Tây, tăng cân bị xem là xấu, còn giảm cân lại được cho là tốt.

Điểm cốt yếu là thế này: nếu "tốt" và "xấu" thực sự hiện hữu một cách tự tính, thì tất cả **mọi người - bất kể nền văn hóa xuất thân - đều sẽ nhận thức giống nhau**. Nhưng thực tế không phải như vậy. **Từ cùng một hoàn cảnh**, có thể phát sinh **những kết luận trái ngược nhau**. Do đó, **vận dụng tuệ giác về tánh Không trong đời sống hằng ngày** có thể giúp chúng ta **tránh khỏi những khổ đau không cần thiết**.

Từ đây, ta có thể thấy rằng ngay cả khi chưa trực chứng tánh Không, thì chỉ cần quán niệm về điều ấy cũng có thể đem lại lợi ích sâu xa. Trong ví dụ đã nêu về vị sếp quở trách, việc quán chiếu về sự phóng chiếu của tâm tuy không làm thay đổi hoàn cảnh bên ngoài, nhưng có thể đoạn dứt khổ thọ nội tâm.

Đức Phật dạy rằng, ngay cả việc chỉ nghe đến tánh Không, hay thậm chí khởi tâm nghi ngờ về tánh Không, cũng đã là đại thiện nghiệp. Vậy thử hình dung lợi lạc lớn lao đến đâu khi ta nghiên cứu và quán niệm sâu xa về tánh Không. Lợi ích khi được tiếp xúc với giáo pháp về tánh Không - chưa nói đến việc tư duy hay thiền quán về nó - là vô lượng. Ngay cả khi nghe pháp với tâm bất thiện, thì việc lắng nghe ấy vẫn có thể mang lại lợi ích. Có một câu chuyện kể rằng: Bồ-tát Văn-thù-sư-lợi (Mañjuśrī) từng thuyết giảng về tánh Không cho một hội chúng đông đảo. Trong số đó, có một nhóm người không hiểu được ý nghĩa của pháp thoại, cảm thấy bực bội nên đã rời khỏi pháp hội, vừa đi vừa phàn nàn rằng bài giảng về tánh Không thật khó hiểu và vô nghĩa. Chính sự phỉ báng ấy khiến họ bị đọa sinh vào địa ngục. Thấy vậy, Tôn giả Xá-lợi-phất (Śāriputra) bạch hỏi Bồ-tát Văn-thù: "Vì sao Ngài lại thuyết giảng tánh Không cho những người mà nay đã bị sinh vào địa ngục?" Bồ-tát Văn-thù đáp: "Những người ấy vốn đã mang nghiệp dẫn họ đến ác đạo, nhưng nhờ có duyên nghe pháp về tánh Không, nên thời gian chịu khổ nơi địa ngục sẽ được rút ngắn lại."

Một ví dụ khác: Trong một chuyến bay nhiều chấn động, một người bạn của tôi - hành khách trên chuyến bay - cảm thấy sợ hãi. Nỗi sợ này khởi lên từ tâm chấp thủ vào một cái "ngã" cố định, khiến anh lo lắng rằng điều gì đó có thể xảy ra với cái "ngã" ấy. Nhưng rồi anh bắt đầu quán chiếu về tánh Không, và truy tìm xem bản chất rắn chắc của "ngã" ấy thực sự nằm ở đâu. Không tìm thấy một cái "ngã" cứng chắc, thật có, nên nỗi sợ trong anh liền lắng xuống. Đó chính là sự ứng dụng thực tiễn của giáo lý về tánh Không. Khi hành giả quán chiếu và phá vỡ cấu trúc tưởng chừng vững chắc của cái "ngã", thì nỗi sợ hãi và lo lắng phát khởi từ đó sẽ tự nhiên lắng dịu.

Khi học *Bát-nhã Tâm Kinh*, mục đích của ta không nên chỉ dừng lại ở việc tích lũy tri thức, mà cần quán chiếu ý nghĩa của giáo lý và ứng dụng vào đời sống hằng ngày. Hãy tự hỏi:

- Tôi có thể vận dụng giáo pháp này như thế nào?
- Giáo lý này giúp tôi hiểu các trải nghiệm trong đời sống như thế nào?

Khi được ứng dụng một cách chân thật, giáo pháp trở nên gắn bó mật thiết với đời sống nội tâm và có năng lực chuyển hóa sâu xa.

Làm rõ về tánh Không

Điều quan trọng là cần xác định rõ điều gì đang bị phủ định khi chúng ta nói đến "tánh Không". Chúng ta **không** hề nói rằng các pháp **không hiện hữu**. Đức Phật **chưa từng dạy rằng các pháp không tồn tại**. Khi nói rằng các pháp **không có tự tánh**, tức là **chúng không hiện hữu một cách độc lập từ phía tự thân**. Ngược lại, các **pháp sinh khởi tùy thuộc vào nhân, duyên, các phần hợp thành** và **sự gán đặt khái niệm** của tâm thức.

Thuật ngữ "**hiện hữu tự tính**" được sử dụng trong tất cả các tông phái Phật giáo, nhưng **mỗi tông phái lại định nghĩa theo một cách khác nhau.** Chính vì vậy mà **dễ nảy sinh sự nhầm lẫn.** Trong tiếng Anh, người ta thường dịch là "intrinsic nature" hoặc "inherent existence", nhưng **Trường phái Trung quán Cụ duyên (Prāsaṅgika)** đưa khái niệm này đến mức độ **vi tế nhất.** Trường phái này chủ trương rằng: nếu các pháp **thật sự hiện hữu tự tính**, thì chúng sẽ **không thể sinh khởi từ nhân duyên, không biến đổi, không hoại diệt**, mà **sẽ tồn tại mãi mãi, bất biến và tĩnh tại.**

Nhưng chúng ta có thể **quan sát rằng mọi hiện tượng đều sinh khởi do nhân và duyên.** Chính vì **sự lệ thuộc ấy** mà **vạn pháp đều rỗng vắng tự tánh.** Nói cách khác: "**Tất cả các pháp nội và ngoại đều rỗng vắng tự tánh vì chúng sinh khởi do duyên.**" Cái thấy này giúp hành giả **tránh rơi vào hai cực đoan: chấp thường (absolutism)** và **chấp đoạn (nihilism).** Thật vậy, nhiều người thường **nghiêng về một trong hai cực đoan** ấy. Khi nghe nói rằng "các pháp hiện hữu", nhiều người **hiểu lầm** rằng điều đó đồng nghĩa với việc các pháp **hiện hữu tự tính** - đây là rơi vào **cực đoan của chấp thường (eternalism).** Ngược lại, khi được dạy rằng "các pháp không hiện hữu tự tính", họ lại **ngộ nhận rằng các pháp hoàn toàn không hiện hữu** - như vậy là rơi vào **cực đoan của đoạn diệt**

(nihilism). Khi một hành giả có thể **thiết lập được cái thấy rằng các pháp tuy có hiện hữu (một cách duyên khởi), nhưng không có tự tánh,** thì **cái thấy ấy được xem là đã đi đúng con đường Trung đạo - vượt thoát khỏi cả hai cực đoan.**

Duyên khởi / Duyên sinh

Photo by Barrett Ward on Unsplash

Tất cả các pháp - cả nội pháp lẫn ngoại pháp - đều không có tự tánh, vì chúng đều sinh khởi một cách duyên khởi.

Duyên khởi (Dependent Arising):

- Phụ thuộc vào nhân và duyên (causes and conditions)
- Phụ thuộc vào các phần hợp thành (parts)
- Tương quan tương duyên (interdependence)
- Phụ thuộc vào danh xưng / sự gán danh (labels / designation)

Có nhiều hình thức duyên khởi khác nhau. Hình thức phổ biến nhất là **sự phụ thuộc vào nhân và duyên.** Ví dụ, cây cỏ sinh trưởng phụ thuộc vào nhiều nguyên nhân như hạt giống, và các duyên như nước, chất dinh dưỡng, v.v...Tất cả các hiện tượng mang tính nhân–quả đều thuộc loại duyên khởi này.

Một hình thức duyên khởi khác là **sự phụ thuộc vào các phần hợp thành.**

Ví dụ, một chiếc xe hơi tồn tại là nhờ các bộ phận như bánh xe, động cơ, v.v.

Nếu không có những bộ phận ấy, thì không thể có cái gọi là "chiếc xe".

Loại thứ ba của duyên khởi được gọi là **"tương tức" hay "tương đãi duyên khởi" (interdependence),** tức là sự tồn tại của một pháp **phụ thuộc hoặc mang tính tương đối so với sự tồn tại của pháp khác**. Ví dụ, các khái niệm "cao" và "thấp" chỉ hiện hữu trong mối quan hệ đối chiếu lẫn nhau: khi ta nói một vật là "thấp", điều đó hàm ý đang so sánh với một vật khác cao hơn. Tương tự, các khái niệm "to" và "nhỏ" cũng chỉ mang ý nghĩa trong tương quan đối đãi.

Cuối cùng là **một loại duyên khởi khác được gọi là "duyên khởi do danh xưng" hay "duyên khởi dựa trên khái niệm."** Ví dụ, chữ cái "A" tồn tại là vì **chúng ta được dạy phải gọi tên như vậy khi thấy một hình dạng gồm những đường nét cụ thể**. Nếu bạn đưa ký tự "A" cho một người chưa từng học bảng chữ cái, người ấy sẽ không nhận ra đó là chữ "A", mà chỉ thấy ba đường kẻ ghép lại với nhau. Điều này minh họa vai trò của **sự gán đặt hoặc quy ước khái niệm bởi tâm thức đối với những gì ta nhận biết.** Nếu không có sự gán danh của tâm, thì **chữ "A" không thể tồn tại**. Sự hiện hữu của nó **phụ thuộc vào một nền tảng vật lý (ba nét kẻ)** và **sự gán đặt của tâm thức rằng đó là "chữ cái A"**.

Những loại duyên khởi đã nêu trên đều nhằm củng cố cái thấy rằng **các pháp không có tự tánh**, mà **sinh khởi do nương tựa hay phụ thuộc vào những yếu tố khác**. Vì vậy, **mọi hiện tượng đều rỗng vắng tự tánh (tức là: đều mang tánh Không).**

Long Thọ (Nāgārjuna) dạy:

"Pháp nào do duyên khởi thì pháp ấy là Không. Pháp ấy được gán danh do duyên khởi. Pháp ấy chính là con đường Trung đạo."

Nói cách khác, **tất cả pháp đều sinh khởi trong sự phụ thuộc vào nhiều yếu tố: nhân, duyên, các phần hợp thành hoặc sự gán đặt khái niệm**. Vạn pháp **đều rỗng không tự tính**.

Và chính nhờ tánh Không, **mọi điều đều có thể xảy ra**

Quán chiếu duyên khởi sẽ dẫn đến sự thấu hiểu Tứ Diệu Đế: Khổ, Tập, Diệt và Đạo.

Kết Luận

Một số tông phái lập luận rằng: nếu các pháp không hiện hữu tự tính, thì sẽ không còn sự phân biệt giữa thiện và ác, giữa công đức và phi đức. Nhưng đây là một sự hiểu lầm.

Việc "chỉ hiện hữu" khác hoàn toàn với "hiện hữu tự tính". Khi chúng ta nói rằng các pháp không hiện hữu tự tính, điều đó không có nghĩa là chúng hoàn toàn không tồn tại. Các pháp vẫn tồn tại - trên bình diện quy ước.

Chúng vẫn vận hành, vẫn có thể mang lại hạnh phúc hoặc khổ đau - nhưng bản chất chúng là không có hiện hữu một cách độc lập. Do đó, hiểu rõ điều này là vô cùng trọng yếu.

Bởi nếu các pháp thật sự tồn tại từ phía tự thân, thì chúng sẽ là cố định, không biến đổi, không già đi, không suy hoại. Chúng sẽ không cần đến nhân duyên mới có thể sinh khởi.

Nhưng chúng ta thấy rằng mọi hiện tượng đều sinh khởi, biến đổi và hoại diệt - tất cả đều do nhân duyên mà thành.

Do đó, kết luận của Trường phái Trung quán Cụ duyên (Prāsaṅgika) là:

Tất cả các pháp đều tồn tại một cách duyên khởi. Vì vậy, tất cả đều là tánh Không. Và chính nhờ mọi pháp đều là tánh Không nên mọi hiện tượng mới có thể sinh khởi.

GIỚI THIỆU VỀ BÁT-NHÃ TÂM KINH

Bát-nhã Tâm Kinh được giảng giải theo ba phần chính: **Phần mở đầu (dẫn nhập), phần chính văn và phần kết luận.** Trong **phần dẫn nhập**, có ba tiểu mục sau: **Tựa đề của kinh, Lời kính lễ (đảnh lễ), Bối cảnh thuyết kinh.**

Phần Dẫn Nhập

- **Tựa đề của bản kinh**

  Ārya bhagavatī prajñāpāramitā hṛdaya (Tinh yếu của Thánh Mẫu: Bát-nhã Ba-la-mật)
- **Lời kính lễ của dịch giả**

  Tôi đảnh lễ Tam Bảo Tôn Quý (Arya Triple Gem)
- **Bối cảnh (duyên khởi)**

  - Phổ thông (chung)
  - Phi thường (riêng biệt)

Tất cả các bản kinh được dịch sang tiếng Tây Tạng đều giữ nguyên tựa đề bằng tiếng Sanskrit. Một trong những lý do cho việc này là nhằm xác lập tính xác thực của bản kinh. Vì Phật giáo khởi nguồn từ Ấn Độ, nên Ấn Độ được xem là cội nguồn thanh tịnh của chánh pháp. Để minh chứng rằng đây là một giáo pháp chân truyền từ Ấn Độ, tựa đề kinh được cố ý giữ nguyên bằng tiếng Sanskrit.

Một lý do khác là để giúp hành giả làm quen với ngôn ngữ Sanskrit và gieo chủng tử trong tâm thức, nhờ đó trong các đời vị lai, việc học Phật pháp sẽ trở nên dễ dàng hơn. Vì có lời dạy rằng tất cả chư Phật sẽ thuyết giảng giáo pháp Đại thừa bằng tiếng Sanskrit, nên tiếng Sanskrit được gọi là ngôn ngữ của chư Thiên - tức là ngôn ngữ của chư Phật.

Bài kệ kính lễ (đảnh lễ) là phần do người dịch soạn ra trong quá trình chuyển dịch kinh từ tiếng Sanskrit sang tiếng Tây Tạng. Mục đích thứ nhất là để tiêu trừ chướng ngại, giúp cho việc dịch kinh được thành tựu viên mãn. Mục đích thứ hai là nhằm xác định bản kinh thuộc về tạng nào trong Tam Tạng Thánh điển của Đức Phật: Kinh tạng (Sūtra), Luận tạng (Abhidharma) hoặc Luật tạng (Vinaya).

Từ bài kệ đảnh lễ, hành giả có thể nhận biết được chủ đề chính yếu của bản kinh:

- Nếu bài kệ đảnh lễ hướng đến tâm Toàn Giác (Nhất Thiết Trí), thì nội dung chính của kinh thuộc về Luật tạng (Giới luật).
- Nếu đảnh lễ Bồ-tát Văn-thù-sư-lợi (Mañjuśrī), thì nội dung chính của kinh thuộc về Trí tuệ (Prajñā) - thường là giáo lý Bát-nhã.
- Những kinh liên quan đến Thiền định (định học) thường đảnh lễ chư Phật và chư Bồ-tát.

Do đó, bài kệ đảnh lễ có vai trò chỉ dẫn, nêu bật trọng tâm của giáo nghĩa trong toàn bộ bản kinh.

Bối cảnh (duyên khởi) là phần trình bày nền tảng dẫn khởi của bản kinh. Có hai loại bối cảnh:

1. Bối cảnh thông thường (common context)
2. Bối cảnh phi thường (uncommon context)

Bối cảnh thông thường (Common Context)

Các điều kiện viên mãn:
– **Thời điểm viên mãn**: *Một thời*
– **Bậc đạo sư viên mãn**: *Đức Phật Thích-ca Mâu-ni*
– **Thính chúng viên mãn**: *Tăng chúng gồm các Tỳ-kheo và chư vị Bồ-tát*
– **Địa điểm viên mãn**: *Núi Linh Thứu (Vulture Peak), thành Vương Xá (Rājagṛha)*
"Như vầy tôi nghe: Một thời Đức Thế Tôn... và đại chúng Bồ-tát..."

Khi bản kinh mở đầu bằng câu: "**Như vầy tôi nghe: Một thời Đức Thế Tôn ngự tại thành Vương Xá, nơi núi Linh Thứu, cùng với đại chúng Tỳ-kheo và đại chúng Bồ-tát...**", thì đoạn này được gọi là "**bối cảnh thông thường**", bởi vì **hầu hết các kinh văn đều khởi đầu theo khuôn mẫu này** - nhằm cung cấp thông tin về **thời điểm, địa điểm, bậc Đạo sư và thính chúng** hiện diện lúc thuyết pháp.

Trong trường hợp của *Bát-nhã Tâm Kinh*, bản kinh này **hội đủ bốn điều kiện viên mãn:**

Thứ nhất, thời điểm viên mãn: Câu mở đầu "**Như vầy tôi nghe...**" cho thấy **tính chất hiếm có của giáo pháp này**. Ngài A-nan, vị đệ tử kết tập kinh tạng, khẳng định rằng **tuy Đức Phật đã thuyết giảng nhiều pháp môn khác nhau**, nhưng giáo pháp của *Bát-nhã Tâm Kinh* **chỉ được thuyết một lần duy nhất**. Điều này cho thấy **sự hy hữu và quý báu đặc biệt** của bản kinh này.

Một cách hiểu khác của câu này là: **Ngài A-nan chỉ nghe một lần nhưng có thể ghi nhớ toàn bộ**, cho thấy **năng lực ghi nhớ phi thường mà Ngài sở hữu.**

Câu **"Đức Thế Tôn đang ngự tại thành Vương Xá, nơi núi Linh Thứu, cùng với đại chúng Tỳ-kheo và đại chúng Bồ-tát..."** thể hiện điều kiện viên mãn thứ hai: **bậc Đạo Sư viên mãn**. Danh xưng *Bhagavān* (Thế Tôn) trong tiếng Sanskrit có nghĩa là:

"Người đã diệt trừ mọi cấu uế và thành tựu viên mãn mọi phẩm hạnh."

Trong bối cảnh này, **Bhagavān** chỉ **Đức Phật Thích-ca Mâu-ni**.

"Núi Linh Thứu" (Vulture's Peak) là điều kiện viên mãn thứ ba - **địa điểm thuyết pháp** nơi Đức Phật truyền dạy bản kinh này. Ngọn núi ấy được gọi là **Linh Thứu** vì hình dáng của nó giống như **một con kên kên**, hoặc giống **đầu kên kên**, hoặc như cảnh tượng một **đàn kên kên tụ hội** trên đỉnh núi. Có nhiều truyền thuyết khác nhau về nguồn gốc tên gọi này, nhưng tất cả đều liên quan đến đặc điểm **hình dáng đỉnh núi** - giống với loài kên kên hoặc **hình ảnh tụ hội** của chúng.

Cuối cùng, cụm từ **"đại chúng Tỳ-kheo và đại chúng Bồ-tát"** chỉ đến điều kiện viên mãn thứ tư - **thính chúng viên mãn**. Điều này cho biết **ai là những vị có mặt trong buổi thuyết pháp**. Như kinh văn đã ghi, vào lúc ấy có một **đại hội quy tụ rất đông chư Tỳ-kheo, chư vị Bồ-tát**, cùng với **các chúng sinh đến từ các cõi giới khác**.

Bối cảnh phi thường (Uncommon Context)
– Đức Phật nhập vào đại định
– Bồ-tát Quán Thế Âm cũng nhập vào thiền định
– Bối cảnh khởi sinh cuộc đối thoại

"Bậc Thế Tôn đã nhập vào chánh định quán sát các pháp, gọi là 'Tướng thâm sâu hiển hiện'. Vào lúc ấy, vị Bồ-tát cao quý Quán Thế Âm (Avalokiteśvara), bậc Đại sĩ đã quán chiếu rõ ràng pháp hành thâm sâu của Bát-nhã Ba-la-mật và... thấy rằng ngay cả năm uẩn cũng không có tự tánh."

Để làm rõ **bối cảnh phi thường**, kinh văn ghi rằng:

"Bậc Thế Tôn đã nhập vào đại định quán sát các hiện tượng sai biệt, gọi là Tướng hiển hiện của thâm sâu. Vào lúc ấy, vị Bồ-tát cao quý Quán Thế Âm, bậc Đại sĩ, đã quán chiếu rõ ràng pháp hành thâm sâu của Bát-nhã Ba-la-mật, và thấy rằng ngay cả năm uẩn cũng đều rỗng không tự tánh."

Đoạn này được gọi là **bối cảnh phi thường** bởi vì đây là **điểm đặc biệt chỉ có trong bản kinh này**. Bối cảnh phi thường cho chúng ta biết hai điều:

(1) **Đức Phật nhập vào thiền định**: Về mặt học thuật, **Đức Phật luôn luôn an trú trong thiền định**; không có thời khắc nào mà Ngài không ở trong định – đây là **một trong vô số công hạnh của bậc Như Lai**. Đức Phật có khả năng **quán chiếu đồng thời hai đế: tục đế và chân đế**. Tuy nhiên, vào thời Đức Phật tại thế ở Ấn Độ, theo truyền thống, **sau khi thọ trai buổi trưa**, Ngài hoặc **nhập định**, hoặc **thuyết pháp**, hoặc **mở cơ hội để các đệ tử được thưa hỏi**. Khi *Bát-nhã Tâm Kinh* được tuyên thuyết, **Đức Phật chọn tiếp tục an trú trong thiền định**. Có vô số loại thiền định mà Đức Phật đã chứng đạt; và vào thời điểm này, Ngài **nhập vào chánh định có tên gọi "Tướng thâm sâu hiển hiện"** - tức **thiền định về tánh Không**. Tánh Không thường được gọi là **"thâm sâu" (gambhīra)**, vì nó **không thể diễn tả bằng ngôn ngữ thế tục** - quá vi tế và vượt ngoài khả năng tư duy thông thường.

(2) **Bồ-tát Quán Thế Âm cũng nhập vào thiền định:** Vào thời điểm ấy, **Bồ-tát Quán Thế Âm cũng nhập vào thiền định về tánh Không** và quán thấy rằng **năm uẩn đều rỗng không tự tính. Vậy, năm uẩn là gì?**

Sắc uẩn (rūpa-skandha)	Bốn đại (đất, nước, lửa, gió), năm căn (mắt, tai, mũi, lưỡi, thân) và các đối tượng của chúng
Thọ uẩn (vedanā-skandha)	Cảm thọ: lạc, khổ, và xả (trung tính)
Tưởng uẩn (saṃjñā-skandha)	Khả năng phân biệt, nhận biết và ghi nhận hình tướng
Hành uẩn (saṃskāra-skandha)	Các tâm sở thiện và bất thiện, các yếu tố tác ý, tư duy, cố gắng v.v.
Thức uẩn (vijñāna-skandha)	Sáu thức: nhãn thức, nhĩ thức, tỵ thức, thiệt thức, thân thức, ý thức

Năm uẩn là một cách để phân loại tất cả các hiện tượng cấu hợp. Mỗi uẩn có một **chức năng riêng biệt**. Giả sử tôi nhìn thấy một chiếc iPhone mới nhất và khởi tâm muốn sở hữu nó. Trong trường hợp này, chúng ta có thể nhận ra **sự vận hành của cả năm uẩn** như sau:

Trước hết, **cơ quan cảm giác** của tôi - **nhãn căn** (con mắt) - phải tiếp xúc với chiếc iPhone (sắc trần). Cả hai yếu tố này đều thuộc về **sắc uẩn**. Tuy nhiên, chỉ sự tiếp xúc giữa nhãn căn và sắc trần vẫn **chưa đủ để nhận biết đối tượng**. Cần có sự hiện diện của **nhãn thức** để nhận diện sự vật - đây chính là vai trò của **thức uẩn**, trong đó nhãn thức là một trong sáu thức.

Tương tự như cách khoa học hiện đại lý giải rằng: **cần có sự phối hợp giữa vật thể, võng mạc và não bộ để tạo nên hình ảnh thị giác**, thì trong Phật giáo, **nhận thức chỉ sinh khởi** khi đầy đủ ba yếu tố: **căn**, **cảnh** và **thức**.

Khi **nhãn thức** khiến tôi thấy chiếc điện thoại, đồng thời các tâm sở khác cũng sinh khởi: tôi có thể **nhận biết và xác định rằng đó là một chiếc iPhone**, đồng thời khởi lên **cảm thọ** - dễ chịu, khó chịu hoặc trung tính - đối với đối tượng ấy. Tâm **nhận biết và phân biệt** đó thuộc về **tưởng uẩn**, còn **cảm thọ** thuộc về **thọ uẩn**.

Từ những cảm thọ phát sinh khi tôi thấy và nhận biết đối tượng, các **thái độ tâm** khác cũng khởi lên - như yêu thích, chán ghét hoặc dửng dưng. Những trạng thái tâm này thuộc về **hành uẩn**, bao gồm các **tâm hành** đa dạng như **thiện, bất thiện hay trung tính**.

Đây là **cách năm uẩn vận hành trong đời sống nội tâm của chúng ta.**

Hiểu được **tánh Không của năm uẩn** - nghĩa là thấy rõ **chúng sinh khởi trong mối tương quan duyên khởi với nhiều yếu tố khác** và không hề có **tự tánh** - là điều **cốt lõi** để thành tựu **Bát-nhã Ba-la-mật (Prajñāpāramitā).**

Kinh văn ghi:

"Khi ấy, dưới sự gia trì của Đức Phật, Tôn giả Xá Lợi Phất bạch với Bồ-tát Quán Thế Âm, bậc Đại sĩ rằng: 'Bạch Bồ-tát, thiện nam tử hay thiện nữ nhân nào phát tâm hành trì pháp tu thâm sâu Bát-nhã Ba-la-mật, thì nên tu học như thế nào?'"

Phần này cho biết **cuộc đối thoại giữa Xá Lợi Phất và Bồ-tát Quán Thế Âm** đã được **khởi sự như thế nào.**

Để hiểu điều đó, trước hết ta cần xét đến **các loại Kinh điển** hay **Giáo pháp (Kāya)** trong lời dạy của Đức Phật. Dù **Giáo pháp được định nghĩa là ngôn từ hay lời dạy của Đức Phật**, nhưng khi nói đến **"lời Phật dạy"**, điều này **không nhất thiết có nghĩa là chính Đức Phật đã trực tiếp thuyết ra những lời ấy bằng miệng.**

Vì thế, **Phật ngữ được phân làm ba loại (Phật ngôn tam chủng).**

Kinh điển (Sūtra): Là gì?

➤ **Là lời dạy hay ngôn từ của Đức Phật**

Gồm ba loại:

- **Lời do chính Đức Phật trực tiếp thuyết giảng**
- **Lời được thuyết với sự cho phép của Đức Phật**
- **Lời phát sinh từ sự gia trì và oai lực của Đức Phật**

Ba loại lời dạy của Đức Phật (Phật ngôn tam chủng)

1. Lời do chính Đức Phật thuyết giảng

Đây là những lời dạy **được Đức Phật trực tiếp tuyên thuyết**. Tức là chính kim khẩu của Ngài đã phát ra lời ấy. Một ví dụ tiêu biểu cho loại "Phật ngôn" này nằm ở phần cuối của *Bát-nhã Tâm Kinh*, khi Đức Phật **tán thán Bồ-tát Quán Thế Âm** vì đã trình bày một cách tuyệt hảo pháp hành Bát-nhã Ba-la-mật: "Tốt lắm! Tốt lắm! Này Thiện nam tử, quả đúng như vậy, chính nên như vậy. Pháp môn thâm sâu Bát-nhã Ba-la-mật cần được hành trì đúng như những gì ông đã tuyên thuyết. Hành trì như vậy, ngay cả chư Như Lai cũng sẽ hoan hỷ."

2. Lời được thuyết với sự cho phép của Đức Phật

Đây không phải là lời do Đức Phật trực tiếp tuyên thuyết, mà là những **lời được Ngài cho phép các vị đệ tử tuyên giảng thay mặt Ngài.** Những lời này được **các vị A-la-hán, như Tôn giả A-nan, ghi nhớ và đưa vào trong quá trình kết tập kinh điển**. Ví dụ minh họa là phần **dẫn nhập** của *Bát-nhã Tâm Kinh*: "Như vầy tôi nghe: Một thời Đức Thế Tôn ngự tại thành Vương Xá, nơi núi Linh Thứu..."

Đoạn này **thiết lập bối cảnh giảng pháp**, thuộc loại **Phật ngôn được thuyết với sự cho phép của Đức Phật**, chứ không phải lời trực tiếp từ kim khẩu của Ngài.

3. Lời dạy phát sinh từ sự gia trì của Đức Phật
Đây là **những lời tuy không do Đức Phật trực tiếp thuyết giảng**, cũng **không phải do Ngài chỉ thị**, mà **được phát khởi nhờ sự gia trì và cảm ứng thầm lặng của Đức Phật**. Đức Phật **im lặng quán chiếu và khởi tác ý gia hộ**, khiến chư vị Bồ-tát hay đệ tử **phát sinh lời giảng** một cách đúng pháp, đúng thời. Trong *Bát-nhã Tâm Kinh*, **phần lớn nội dung** thuộc loại Phật ngôn này. Cụ thể là **cuộc đối thoại giữa Tôn giả Xá-lợi-phất và Bồ-tát Quán Thế Âm không xuất phát từ ý chí tự thân của hai vị**, mà là **do Đức Phật thầm gia trì** để các ngài **khởi thoại đúng như ý chỉ giáo pháp** của Ngài. Một ví dụ khác là *KINH THÁNH TỊCH BẠCH CÁI (Ārya Sitātapatrā Sūtra)*, được **tuyên thuyết từ đảnh tướng (uṣṇīṣa)** của Đức Phật khi Ngài đang an trú tại **cõi Trời Ba Mươi Ba (Trāyastriṃśa)**. Trong thời gian an trú tại cõi Trời Ba Mươi Ba, Đức Phật không thuyết pháp bằng khẩu ngữ, vì trước đó Ngài đã hứa với Tôn giả A-nan rằng sẽ không giảng pháp khi A-nan không có mặt.

Khi ấy, Tôn giả A-nan vẫn chưa chứng đắc **thần thông để có thể vãng thăng đến cõi trời này**, nên buộc phải ở lại nhân gian. Do đó, **tất cả những lời dạy trong giai đoạn ấy đều được truyền đạt qua các phương tiện khác**, thay vì lời nói khẩu ngữ trực tiếp của Đức Phật.

PHẦN CHÍNH VĂN CỦA KINH

Chính văn của *Bát-nhã Tâm Kinh* được phân chia thành ba tiểu mục chính sau:

1. **Câu hỏi của Tôn giả Xá-lợi-phất liên quan đến pháp Bát-nhã Ba-la-mật**

2. **Lời đáp của Bồ-tát Quán Thế Âm - (trình bày pháp Bát-nhã Ba-la-mật)**

3. **Sự xác nhận và lời tuyên dương hoan hỷ của Đức Phật**

1. Câu hỏi của Xá-lợi-phất về pháp môn Bát-nhã Ba-la-mật

"Khi ấy, dưới sự cảm ứng của Đức Phật, Tôn giả Xá-lợi-phất bạch cùng Bồ-tát Quán Thế Âm, bậc Đại sĩ tôn quý rằng:

'Bạch Bồ-tát, thiện nam tử hay thiện nữ nhân nào phát nguyện hành trì pháp môn thâm sâu Bát-nhã Ba-la-mật, thì nên tu học như thế nào?'"

Đây là **khởi điểm của phần chính văn**, nơi **Xá-lợi-phất - vị đệ tử trí tuệ bậc nhất của Đức Phật** - thay mặt đại chúng nêu lên câu hỏi **cốt lõi liên quan đến pháp hành Bát-nhã.**

Câu hỏi này **mở đường cho toàn bộ phần giảng pháp sau đó của Bồ-tát Quán Thế Âm**, làm rõ **cách thực hành trí tuệ thâm sâu**, dẫn đến **chứng ngộ tính không** và **thành tựu Bát-nhã Ba-la-mật.**

Câu hỏi của Tôn giả Xá-lợi-phất về pháp môn Bát-nhã Ba-la-mật

"Khi ấy, dưới sự cảm ứng của Đức Phật, Tôn giả Xá-lợi-phất bạch cùng Bồ-tát Quán Thế Âm, bậc Đại sĩ rằng:
'Bạch Bồ-tát, thiện nam tử hay thiện nữ nhân nào muốn hành trì pháp môn thâm sâu Bát-nhã Ba-la-mật thì nên tu học như thế nào?'"

Câu hỏi của Tôn giả Xá-lợi-phất về pháp môn Bát-nhã Ba-la-mật

"Khi ấy, dưới sự cảm ứng của Đức Phật, Tôn giả Xá-lợi-phất bạch cùng Bồ-tát Quán Thế Âm, bậc Đại sĩ rằng:

'Bạch Bồ-tát, thiện nam tử hay thiện nữ nhân nào muốn hành trì pháp môn thâm sâu Bát-nhã Ba-la-mật thì nên tu học như thế nào?'"

Câu hỏi mà Tôn giả Xá-lợi-phất nêu lên với Bồ-tát Quán Tự Tại là: *"Làm thế nào để một thiện nam tử hay thiện nữ nhân tu tập pháp môn thâm sâu Bát-nhã Ba-la-mật?"* Việc sử dụng cụm từ **"thiện nam tử" và "thiện nữ nhân"** mang một ý nghĩa sâu xa. Theo quan điểm Phật giáo, tất cả chúng sinh-kể cả những sinh vật nhỏ bé như côn trùng hay những người phạm trọng tội như kẻ sát nhân hàng loạt-đều có **Phật tánh**, tức là hạt giống thanh tịnh, một tiềm năng giác ngộ sẵn có nơi tự tánh. Tuy nhiên, hạt giống ấy cần được **nuôi dưỡng và trưởng thành (chín muồi)** thì mới có thể khởi hành trên con đường giác ngộ. Một ví dụ minh họa xác đáng là **thỏi vàng bị phủ đầy bùn đất**: Xét về bản chất và giá trị, vàng dính bùn và vàng sáng bóng không có gì sai biệt. Chỉ cần gột sạch lớp bùn đất, thì ánh sáng thật sự của vàng sẽ hiển lộ. Cũng vậy, mọi chúng sinh phàm phu đều như **thỏi vàng lấm bẩn.** Tất cả chúng ta đều có tiềm năng thành tựu giác ngộ viên mãn; chỉ là hiện tại đang bị che phủ bởi lớp phiền não dày đặc. Thông qua sự thực hành, chúng ta có thể dần dần gỡ bỏ những lớp phiền não ấy và cuối cùng đạt đến sự giải thoát hoàn toàn khỏi mọi lậu hoặc. Vì vậy, cụm từ **"thiện nam tử"** và **"thiện nữ nhân"** ở đây chỉ những người nơi đó **Phật tánh đã được thành thục.** Những ai đã phát khởi và nuôi dưỡng **tâm đại bi** được xem là những người mà Phật tánh đã chín muồi.

Một cách hiểu khác về cụm từ "thiện nam tử, thiện nữ nhân" là: chỉ những người có **căn cơ thích hợp** để tiếp nhận giáo pháp về tánh Không (*śūnyatā*). Giáo lý này không dễ tiếp nhận với tất cả mọi người - có người khi nghe giảng về tánh Không thì sinh tâm lo lắng, bất an, thậm chí sợ hãi. Vì vậy, cụm từ trên ám chỉ những ai thực sự là **pháp khí xứng đáng** để thọ nhận giáo pháp thâm sâu về Bát-nhã Ba-la-mật. **Tôn giả Nguyệt Xứng (Candrakīrti)**, trong tác phẩm *Nhập Trung Quán Luận* (*Madhyamakāvatāra*), có nói: "Những ai có nhân duyên sâu dày với tánh Không, khi nghe giảng pháp ấy sẽ tự nhiên xúc động rơi lệ." Việc kinh văn sử dụng song song hai từ "thiện nam tử" và "thiện nữ nhân" hàm ý rõ ràng rằng trong việc tu tập pháp môn Bát-nhã Ba-la-mật và chứng đắc giác ngộ, **không hề có sự phân biệt giới tính**. Dù vào thời Đức Phật tại Ấn Độ, định kiến giới tính còn rất sâu nặng, nhưng Đức Phật đã tuyên thuyết minh bạch rằng: **bất kỳ ai - nam hay nữ - đều có thể tu học Bát-nhã Ba-la-mật và chứng thành Phật quả.**

2. Lời đáp của Bồ-tát Quán Tự Tại: Trình bày về pháp môn Bát-nhã Ba-la-mật và Ngũ đạo tu chứng trong Đại thừa

"Sau khi điều này được nói, Thánh giả Quán Tự Tại, vị Bồ-tát, bậc Đại sĩ, liền nói với Tôn giả Xá Lợi Phất: 'Này Xá Lợi Phất, bất kỳ thiện nam tử hay thiện nữ nhân nào phát tâm hành trì pháp môn thâm sâu Bát-nhã Ba-la-mật thì nên quán chiếu như vầy: Họ nên thấy một cách viên mãn rằng ngay cả năm uẩn cũng đều không có tự tính...Chân ngôn của Bát-nhã Ba-la-mật được tuyên thuyết: **tadyathā gate gate pāragate pārasaṃgate bodhi svāhā!** Này Xá Lợi Phất, các vị Bồ-tát, bậc Đại sĩ, nên tu học Bát-nhã Ba-la-mật như vậy.'"

Kể từ đoạn này, Bồ-tát Quán Tự Tại trình bày phương pháp hành trì Bát-nhã Ba-la-mật theo hai hình thức: một bản trình bày chi tiết dành cho những người có trí tuệ thông thường, một bản trình bày súc tích dành cho những người có đại trí. Phần trình bày chi tiết bao gồm các pháp hành cụ thể được thiết lập theo tiến trình năm đạo trong Đại thừa. Vậy **năm đạo của Đại thừa là gì?**

Ngũ Đạo trong Đại Thừa (The Five Mahayana Paths)

Đạo Tư Lương (Path of Accumulation) – Phát khởi Bồ-đề tâm (Bodhicitta)

↑

Đạo Gia Hạnh (Path of Preparation) – Hợp nhất giữa Chỉ và Quán (Định và Tuệ)

↑

Đạo Kiến (Path of Seeing) – Trực chứngTánh Không (sự chứng ngộ trực tiếp về Không tính)

↑

Đạo Tu (Path of Meditation) – Đối trị trực tiếp các chướng ngại còn tồn tại của đạo tu

↑

Đạo Vô Học (Path of No More Learning) – Thành tựu Phật quả (Buddhahood)

Để trở thành một vị Phật, hành giả cần phải "tuần tự bước lên" nấc thang của **Ngũ đạo trong Đại thừa**. Nói cách khác, cần phải tu tập theo con đường này để đạt đến những tầng bậc chứng ngộ nhất định. Những tầng bậc đó giống như những cột mốc đánh dấu sự thành tựu trên hành trình tiến đến giác ngộ: **Đạo Tư Lương, Đạo Gia Hạnh, Đạo Kiến, Đạo Tu** và **Đạo Vô Học.**

(1) Đạo Tư Lương (Path of Accumulation):

Khi một hành giả Đại thừa lần đầu tiên phát khởi Bồ-đề tâm một cách tự nhiên và liên tục, vị ấy đã bước vào Đạo Tư Lương. Do phát khởi Bồ-đề tâm, từ thời điểm đó trở đi, mọi pháp tu đều được thúc đẩy bởi tâm nguyện vị tha này, khiến cho mọi công đức tích tập đều trở nên vô cùng lớn mạnh. Do vậy, con đường này được gọi là Đạo Tư Lương. Tuy nhiên, ở giai đoạn này, hành giả có thể đã hoặc chưa trực ngộ được tánh Không.

(2) Đạo Gia Hạnh (Path of Preparation):

Một hành giả ở giai đoạn Đạo Tư Lương sẽ bắt đầu thực hành cả hai loại thiền: thiền định nhất tâm (Chỉ) và thiền quán chiếu (Quán). Dần dần, hành giả đạt được tam-ma-địa (định tĩnh) và minh sát (quán chiếu về tánh Không). Khi đạt được sự hợp nhất giữa Chỉ và Quán, hành giả bước vào Đạo Gia Hạnh. Ở giai đoạn này, hành giả có thể "thấy" tánh Không ở cấp độ khái niệm. Tuy nhiên, đó chưa phải là cái thấy trực tiếp, nên vẫn thiếu sự minh bạch-giống như thấy tánh Không qua một tấm màn che. Việc thường xuyên thiền quán về tánh Không với định nhất tâm sẽ chuẩn bị cho hành giả đạt được cái thấy trực tiếp về tánh Không. Vì vậy, giai đoạn này được gọi là Đạo Gia Hạnh.

(3) Đạo Kiến (Path of Seeing):

Một hành giả ở giai đoạn Đạo Gia Hạnh sẽ liên tục thiền quán về tánh Không cho đến khi sự hiểu biết và chứng ngộ về tánh Không trở nên minh bạch đến mức dường như không còn phân biệt giữa tánh Không và tâm thức đang nhận biết nó. Khi đạt đến cái thấy sâu sắc ấy, hành giả chứng đắc cái thấy trực tiếp về tánh Không, bước vào Đạo Kiến và trở thành bậc Thánh (*Ārya*).

(4) Đạo Tu (Path of Meditation):

Sau khi đã đạt được cái thấy trực tiếp về tánh Không, hành giả bước vào đạo tu và tiếp tục thiền quán về tánh Không nhằm tận diệt vô minh và các chủng tử nhiễm ô vi tế - cụ thể là các chấp thủ vi tế vào tự tính: chấp ngã, chấp pháp, và chấp hữu nội tại. Những chướng ngại đặc biệt này chính là các "sở đoạn" mà đạo tu cần đoạn trừ. Khoảng thời gian từ khi bước vào đạo tu cho đến lúc tận diệt hoàn toàn các sở đoạn này (tức là các vi tế chấp vào sự hiện hữu tự tính), được gọi là giai đoạn của đạo tu. Khi đã đoạn trừ trọn vẹn các sở đoạn ấy, hành giả sẽ bước vào đạo vô học.

(5) Đạo Vô Học (Path of No More Learning):

Đây là giai đoạn hành giả thành tựu Phật quả. Ở mức này, hành giả đã đoạn trừ hoàn toàn mọi chướng ngại thô và vi tế, đồng thời viên mãn tất cả các phẩm tính giác ngộ. Đây là cảnh giới toàn tri, nên được gọi là "đạo vô học" - tức con đường không còn điều gì cần phải học nữa.

Tu Tập theo Đạo Tư Lương và Đạo Gia Hạnh:

TÂM KINH – PHẨM 2

"Khi điều ấy được nói ra, thánh giả Quán Tự Tại, vị Bồ-tát, bậc Đại sĩ, đã thưa với tôn giả Xá Lợi Phất rằng: 'Xá Lợi Phất, bất kỳ thiện nam tử hay thiện nữ nhân nào muốn hành trì pháp môn thâm sâu Bát-nhã Ba-la-mật-đa, nên quán chiếu một cách rõ ràng như sau:'"

TÂM KINH – PHẨM 3

"Họ nên quán chiếu một cách viên mãn rằng ngay cả năm uẩn cũng đều không có tự tính. Sắc tức là Không, Không tức là Sắc; Không chẳng khác Sắc, Sắc chẳng khác Không. Cũng như vậy: Thọ, Tưởng, Hành, Thức đều là Không."

Quán Tự Tại bắt đầu phần trả lời bằng cách khẳng định rằng bất kỳ ai muốn hành trì pháp môn thâm sâu Bát-nhã Ba-la-mật-đa đều cần phải quán chiếu một cách rõ ràng rằng ngay cả năm uẩn cũng không có tự tính. Từ "ngay cả" (even) nhằm nhấn mạnh tầm quan trọng của việc chứng ngộ vô ngã của ngã thể (ở đây "ngã thể" ám chỉ khái niệm hay danh xưng "tôi") cũng như vô ngã của các pháp (ở đây "pháp" là chỉ cho các uẩn). Lý do là: mặc dù ta có thể hiểu bằng lý trí, thậm chí có thể có tri kiến chứng ngộ về tánh Không của ngã thể, nhưng chừng nào ta vẫn còn chấp thủ vào ý niệm rằng các uẩn có bản thể độc lập, thì tập khí chấp ngã vẫn chưa được đoạn trừ. Niềm tin vào tự tính cố hữu chính là vô minh, và khi sống dựa trên nền tảng sai lầm này, tất yếu sẽ tạo nghiệp và từ đó dẫn đến luân hồi sinh tử. Do đó, chỉ chứng ngộ vô ngã của ngã thể là chưa đủ để thoát khỏi luân hồi, chứ chưa nói đến việc đạt đến quả vị giác ngộ.

Để khai triển thêm lời đáp, Bồ-tát Quán Tự Tại nói tiếp: "Sắc là Không, Không tức là Sắc; Không chẳng khác Sắc, Sắc cũng chẳng khác Không."

Hãy cùng tìm hiểu bốn mệnh đề này - đây chính là cốt lõi của Bát-nhã Tâm Kinh, được gọi là "bốn phương diện quán chiếu tánh Không". Trong đó, tương đối dễ hiểu câu đầu tiên: "Sắc tức là Không." Chúng ta đã bàn rằng mọi pháp đều tồn tại dựa vào nhân duyên, các phần cấu thành, và sự giả lập của tâm thức. Nếu sự hiện hữu của một pháp phụ thuộc vào các yếu tố khác, thì theo lý suy luận, điều đó phủ định sự tồn tại độc lập. Điều này áp dụng cho cả sắc pháp.

Kinh Vấn Anavatapta dạy rõ rằng:

"Cái gì do nhân duyên sinh thì vốn không sinh,
Vì không có sự khởi sinh tự tính.
Cái gì tùy thuộc nơi duyên thì được tuyên thuyết là Không.
Ai liễu tri tánh Không ấy thì an trú trong tịch tĩnh."

Vì vậy, Bồ-tát Quán Tự Tại nói rằng, cũng như mọi pháp khác, "sắc" cũng sinh khởi do nhân và duyên, nên không có sự tồn tại độc lập. Do đó, sắc vốn không có tự tính (tự tính cố hữu). Chính sự vắng mặt của tự tính ấy chính là tánh Không của sắc. Điều này áp dụng cho tất cả các pháp. Ví dụ, một chiếc xe không có tự tính cố hữu-và đó chính là tánh Không của chiếc xe. Chiếc xe tồn tại như một hiện tượng duyên khởi - tức là dựa trên các bộ phận cấu thành, nhân và duyên, cùng sự gán nhãn bởi tâm thức - chứ không hiện hữu như một "chiếc xe" tồn tại độc lập, có tự tính cố hữu. Tánh Không của chiếc xe không gì khác hơn là bản tánh tối hậu của nó. Nói cách khác, sự vắng mặt tự tính cố hữu chính là bản tánh tối hậu hay phương diện hiện hữu tối hậu của chiếc xe. Hay nói cách khác, tánh Không chính là một đặc tướng - một phương diện - của chiếc xe.

Hai Đế – The Two Truths:

Hai phương diện hiện hữu – Two modes of being:

- Hiện hữu tối hậu (The ultimate mode of being):
  Chính là sự vắng mặt của tính tồn tại độc lập – tức là tánh Không (śūnyatā).

- Hiện hữu quy ước (The conventional mode of being):
  Chính là sự gán đặt đơn thuần bởi tâm thức – tức là hiện tượng chỉ tồn tại thông qua tâm phân biệt và quy ước danh xưng.

Đây là hai phương diện của cùng một pháp, giống như hai mặt của một đồng tiền. Một hiện tượng tồn tại đúng đắn cần đồng thời mang đủ hai mặt này: hiện hữu trong thế giới quy ước và trống rỗng tự tính ở cấp độ tối hậu.

Một phương diện khác của sắc là cách hiện hữu quy ước của nó. Tuy sắc không tồn tại một cách cố hữu, nhưng nó vẫn có sự hiện hữu. Sự hiện hữu này là nhờ sự gán đặt đơn thuần của tâm thức. Sắc chỉ là một sự gán đặt bởi tâm thì chính là chân lý tục đế - tức phương diện quy ước của sắc. Mọi pháp đều có hai phương diện hiện hữu như vậy, thường được gọi là nhị đế. Hai cách hiện hữu của sắc tuy dường như tách biệt, nhưng trên thực tế là một. Chúng như hai mặt của cùng một đồng xu..

Câu thứ hai nói rằng: "Không tức là sắc." Vậy sắc là gì? Sắc chỉ là một sự gán đặt đơn thuần của tâm thức lên một căn bản, là nhãn hiệu được đặt lên một tổng thể các thành phần hợp lại. Ví dụ, "chiếc xe" là một danh xưng được gán lên sự kết hợp của nhiều bộ phận cụ thể. Việc gán danh như vậy chỉ khả hữu bởi vì chiếc xe không có sự tồn tại độc lập. Nếu chiếc xe có bản chất hoặc thực thể riêng biệt độc lập, thì sự gán đặt bởi tâm sẽ không thể thực hiện được. Theo cách đó, tánh Không chính là nền tảng cho sự hiện hữu của chiếc xe.

Hãy nhìn vào các nút thắt dây trong hình. Từ một sợi dây, ta có thể tạo ra vô số kiểu nút khác nhau. Điều này chỉ khả thi vì sợi dây có tính mềm dẻo và linh hoạt. Nếu dây cứng và không thể uốn cong, thì việc tạo ra nhiều hình dạng nút khác nhau là điều bất khả. Chính tính mềm dẻo ấy là nền tảng cho mọi hình dạng nút thắt có thể hình dung. Theo cách ấy, các nút thắt khác nhau chính là những biểu hiện đa dạng của cùng một sợi dây.

Tương tự, sắc là sự hiển lộ của tánh Không. Bởi vì các pháp không có tự tính nơi chính chúng, nên mới có thể hiện khởi thành muôn hình tướng. Thật vậy, tất cả các pháp quy ước đều là sự hiển lộ hoặc biểu hiện của tánh Không. Chính nhờ sắc là Không mà phương diện quy ước của sắc mới có thể tồn tại. Do đó, Không tức là sắc.

Hai mệnh đề thứ ba và thứ tư nhấn mạnh mối liên hệ giữa hai phương diện tồn tại của một pháp. Hai phương diện này tuy dường như sai biệt, nhưng thực chất là một - như hai mặt của cùng một đồng xu. Chẳng hạn, bản tánh tối hậu của chiếc xe là tánh Không, tức là sự vắng mặt của tự tính cố hữu. Sự hiện hữu quy ước của nó chỉ là một nhãn hiệu được tâm thức gán đặt lên một nền tảng vốn không có tự tính. Bốn mệnh đề trên-"Sắc tức là Không, Không tức là Sắc; Sắc chẳng khác Không, Không chẳng khác Sắc"-là phương pháp bốn chiều để quán chiếu tánh Không, và cần được áp dụng tương tự với bốn uẩn còn lại. Do đó, trong Kinh dạy: "Cảm thọ, tưởng, hành và thức cũng đều là Không." Ví dụ: Cảm thọ tức là Không, Không tức là cảm thọ, Không chẳng khác cảm thọ, cảm thọ cũng chẳng khác Không.

Tu tập theo Đạo Kiến

Kinh văn chép:

"Cho nên, này Xá-lợi-phất, tất cả các pháp đều là Không; không có tự tánh; không sinh, không diệt; không nhiễm, không tịnh; không thiếu, không đủ."

Đoạn kinh này cho thấy cách thức mà một hành giả ở giai đoạn Đạo Kiến nên hành trì Bát-nhã Ba-la-mật-đa. Bồ-tát Quán Tự Tại dạy rằng người ở giai đoạn này nên thực hành cái gọi là ba môn giải thoát-tức là phương pháp quán chiếu tánh Không dưới ba phương diện khác nhau.

Ba môn giải thoát:

- Ở phương diện quy ước, tám đặc tính vẫn hiện hữu.
- Ở phương diện tối hậu, chỉ có sự vắng mặt của các đặc tính này:

Đặc tính (định tính) – môn Không (bản chất của sự vật)
Sinh khởi – môn Vô tướng (nguyên nhân)
Diệt tận – môn Vô tướng (nguyên nhân)
Ô nhiễm – môn Vô tướng (nguyên nhân)
Thanh tịnh – môn Vô tướng (nguyên nhân)
Giảm – môn Vô nguyện (kết quả)
Tăng – môn Vô nguyện (kết quả)
→ Các đặc tính này không tồn tại như là bản chất tối hậu của các pháp.

Môn Không: Cách thứ nhất là quán chiếu tánh Không từ chính lập trường của sự Không. Bồ-tát Quán Tự Tại dạy rằng: sau khi đã quán chiếu năm uẩn bằng phương pháp phân tích bốn phần, ta nên quán chiếu tất cả các pháp theo cách ấy. Khi làm như vậy, ta sẽ đi đến kết luận rằng: tất cả các pháp đều là Không. Ngay cả những đặc tính định danh của các pháp cũng rỗng vắng tự tính. Ở cấp độ quy ước, vẫn có các tướng trạng phân biệt – tức là các tướng riêng và tướng chung. Tuy nhiên, ở cấp độ tối hậu, không có đặc tính nào tồn tại một cách cố hữu.

Vô Tướng Môn: Phương pháp thứ hai để quán chiếu tánh Không là nhìn từ góc độ nhân-tức nguyên nhân dẫn đến sự xuất hiện của các pháp. Ở cấp độ quy ước, có sự sinh và diệt, hiện khởi và biến mất của các pháp. Mọi sự vật đều có khởi điểm và kết thúc (do các duyên như nhân tố, bộ phận cấu thành và sự gán đặt của tâm thức kết hợp mà thành). Tuy nhiên, chính vì sự nương tựa vào nhiều yếu tố như vậy nên ở cấp độ tối hậu, không có sự sinh khởi hay diệt tận một cách độc lập. Không có pháp nào tự sinh, cũng không có pháp nào tự diệt. Tương tự, các nhiễm ô cần được đoạn trừ và các phẩm hạnh thanh tịnh cần được tu tập-chẳng hạn như giải thoát và quả vị Phật-chỉ tồn tại trên phương diện thực tại quy ước. Không có sự đoạn trừ nhiễm ô hay tu tập các phẩm hạnh thanh tịnh nào mang tính cố hữu.

Cửa Vô Nguyện: Cách thứ ba là quán chiếu tánh Không từ phương diện kết quả. Ở cấp độ quy ước, khi chúng ta áp dụng các pháp đối trị đối với những phiền não như sân hận, tham ái và vô minh, các phiền não này sẽ dần dần suy giảm. Tương tự, các phẩm hạnh như từ bi, thiện tâm, nhẫn nhục có thể được nuôi dưỡng và thành tựu viên mãn. Do vậy, sự suy giảm của các nhiễm ô và sự tăng trưởng của các phẩm hạnh tích cực là điều có mặt ở bình diện quy ước. Tuy nhiên, khi đặt chúng dưới sự phân tích tối hậu, ta thấy rằng tất cả đều là sản phẩm của duyên khởi, chứ không tồn tại một cách cố hữu. Vì vậy, không có pháp nào có thể vượt qua được sự khảo sát tối hậu - do đó, tất cả các pháp đều rỗng không tự tính.

Tu tập theo Đạo Tu (Thiền Định)

Để chỉ ra cách hành trì trên Đạo Tu, Bồ-tát Quán Tự Tại tiếp tục:

"Vì vậy, này Shariputra, trong tánh Không không có sắc, không có thọ, không có tưởng, không có hành, không có thức. Không có nhãn, nhĩ, tỷ, thiệt, thân, ý. Không có sắc, thanh, hương, vị, xúc, pháp." Không có nhãn giới, cho đến không có ý thức giới, bao gồm cả không có thức giới của ý. Không có vô minh, cũng không có sự diệt tận của vô minh; cho đến không có già chết, cũng không có sự diệt tận của già chết. Tương tự như vậy, không có khổ, tập, diệt, đạo; không có trí, không có chứng đắc, thậm chí cũng không có cả phi chứng đắc.

Trong đoạn kinh này, có nhiều nhóm pháp đối tượng được quán chiếu, do đó trước hết cần được triển khai cho rõ ràng. Kinh văn khởi đầu với năm uẩn, và lần lượt phủ định từng uẩn bằng cách tuyên thuyết: "không có sắc, không có thọ", v.v. Năm uẩn thực ra vẫn hiện hữu ở cấp độ quy ước, nhưng điều được phủ định ở đây chính là: chúng không tồn tại từ quan điểm của một hành giả đang ở giai đoạn Đạo Tu, đang an trụ sâu trong thiền quán về tánh Không. Vì hành giả ở giai đoạn này đã chứng ngộ trực tiếp tánh Không, nên khi an trú trong thiền định, trong nhận thức của họ không có gì hiện khởi ngoài tánh Không (chính là sự vắng mặt của tự tính). Do đó, dưới cái nhìn của hành giả đang nhập định, không có sắc, thọ, tưởng, hành, thức, v.v.

Tiếp theo đó, kinh văn liệt kê **18 giới** (hay 18 yếu tố), bao gồm:

- **6 trần cảnh (đối tượng nhận thức):** sắc, thanh, hương, vị, xúc, pháp;
- **6 căn (giác quan):** nhãn căn, nhĩ căn, tị căn, thiệt căn, thân căn, ý căn;

- **6 thức (thức nhận biết):** nhãn thức, nhĩ thức, tị thức, thiệt thức, thân thức, ý thức.

18 giới (18 yếu tố):

- **6 thức:** nhãn thức, nhĩ thức, tị thức, thiệt thức, thân thức, ý thức
- **6 căn (giác quan):** nhãn căn, nhĩ căn, tị căn, thiệt căn, thân căn, ý căn
- **6 trần cảnh (đối tượng nhận thức):** sắc, thanh, hương, vị, xúc, pháp

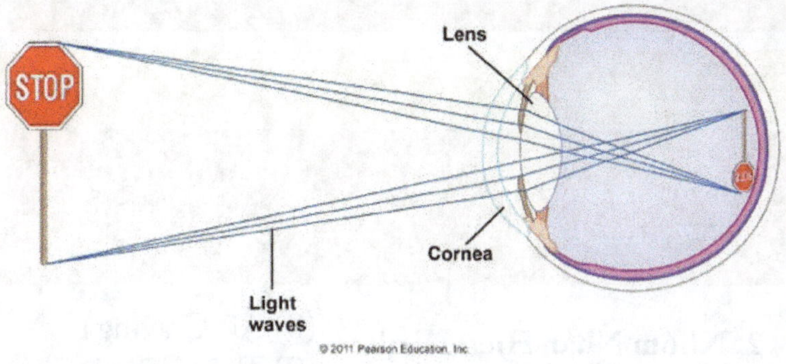

Image → Retina → Primary visual cortex

Hình minh họa là sơ đồ về tiến trình nhận thức thị giác – từ hình ảnh bên ngoài → ánh sáng chiếu vào võng mạc → truyền đến vỏ não thị giác (primary visual cortex) – minh hoạ sự phối hợp giữa trần cảnh (đối tượng), căn (giác quan) và thức (ý thức nhận biết). Đây là một ví dụ sinh lý học hiện đại để biểu thị cách thức các thành tố phối hợp tạo ra nhận thức trong dòng tương tục. Tuy nhiên, trong quán chiếu theo tuệ giác Bát-nhã, hành giả thấy rằng tất cả các yếu tố này đều không có tự tính cố hữu – nghĩa là không hiện hữu một cách độc lập, mà chỉ tồn tại do duyên hợp. Vì thế, trong thiền định về tánh Không, chúng đều bị phủ nhận như là các thực thể có tự tính độc lập.

Bồ-tát Quán Tự Tại dạy rằng tất cả 18 giới này không hiện khởi trong nhận thức của các hành giả đang nhập định và an trụ trong thiền quán về tánh Không. Mười hai chi phần của Duyên khởi, Tứ Thánh Đế, trí tuệ và quả chứng là một nhóm pháp khác được ngài liệt kê. Trên phương diện quy ước, Mười hai nhân duyên, Tứ Thánh Đế và quả chứng vẫn tồn tại, nhưng đối với hành giả đang an trú trong trực giác về tánh Không, chúng đều không có sự hiện hữu tự tính. Đây là một cách lý giải những dòng Kinh này như là phương pháp tu tập trong giai đoạn của Đạo Tu Thiền định.

12 chi phần của duyên khởi (Thập nhị nhân duyên)	
Nhóm Nhân Dẫn (Projecting Factors):	(1) Vô minh (Ignorance) (2) Hành (Hành nghiệp) (Compounded Karma) (3) Thức (Consciousness)
2. Nhóm Nhân Hiện Hành (Actualizing Factors):	(8) Ái (Craving) (9) Thủ (Grasping) (10) Hữu (Existence)
3. Nhóm Quả (Results):	(4) Danh và sắc (Name & Form) (5) Lục nhập (Six sources) (6) Xúc (Contact) (7) Thọ (Feeling) (11) Sinh (Birth) (12) Lão tử (Aging & Death)

Vì con đường tu tập thiền định là một tiến trình dài, nên đòi hỏi sự hành trì liên tục và lặp đi lặp lại trong thiền quán về tánh Không. Để minh thị điều này, Bồ tát Quán Thế Âm đã liệt kê nhiều ví dụ và đối tượng nhằm quán chiếu bản tánh tối hậu, tức tánh Không, của chúng. Một cách hiểu khác của đoạn trên là: tất cả các nhóm đối tượng vừa nêu đều có sự hiện hữu theo phương diện quy ước, nhưng không hiện hữu một cách tự tính hay độc lập. Năm uẩn, mười tám giới, mười hai chi phần của duyên khởi và cả sự chứng đắc đều phụ thuộc vào nhân và duyên, nên chúng không có tự tính hay bản chất độc lập.

Tu tập theo Đạo Vô Học

Kinh văn viết:

> Tâm kinh phẩm 5: Vì vậy, này Xá-lợi-phất, do các vị Bồ-tát không có sở đắc nào, nên họ nương vào Bát-nhã Ba-la-mật-đa này và an trụ nơi đó. Vì tâm không còn chướng ngại, nên không có sợ hãi; vượt hẳn mọi điên đảo mộng tưởng, họ rốt ráo đạt đến niết-bàn.

"Vì vậy, này Xá-lợi-phất, do các vị Bồ-tát không có sở đắc nào, nên họ nương vào Bát-nhã Ba-la-mật-đa này và an trụ nơi đó."

Bồ-tát Quán Tự Tại dạy rằng các vị Bồ-tát, sau khi đã quán chiếu tánh Không của tất cả các pháp - kể cả các sở đắc rốt ráo - nên an trụ trong sự chứng ngộ trực tiếp về tánh Không ấy. Đây chính là cách thức hành trì Bát-nhã Ba-la-mật-đa thâm sâu, và vì vậy, các vị nên chuyên tâm an trụ nơi đó.

Tiếp theo, Bồ-tát Quán Tự Tại dạy rằng việc hành trì như vậy rốt cuộc sẽ đoạn trừ được **vô minh chấp ngã**-tức là sự chấp vào tính tồn tại cố hữu của ngã và của các pháp-qua đó tiêu trừ được **hai chướng ngại**: phiền não chướng và sở tri chướng. Nhờ đó, nỗi **sợ hãi sinh khởi từ chấp ngã sẽ không còn nữa**; hành giả sẽ **vượt thoát khỏi lưới lầm tưởng sai lầm** và đạt đến **bờ kia của Niết-bàn**, tức là thành tựu **Phật quả**.

Như đoạn kinh văn tiếp theo khẳng định:

"Tất cả chư Phật trong ba đời cũng y cứ vào Bát-nhã Ba-la-mật thâm sâu này mà đạt đến chứng đắc Vô Thượng Chánh Đẳng Chánh Giác."

Đây chính là con đường mà chư Phật ba đời - **quá khứ, hiện tại và tương lai** đã thành tựu giác ngộ – bằng cách **hành trì và nương tựa vào trí tuệ Ba-la-mật thâm sâu** để thực hành và chứng đắc.

Trình bày ngắn gọn dưới hình thức thần chú

"Vì vậy, nên biết rằng thần chú của Bát-nhã Ba-la-mật-thần chú của đại trí tuệ, thần chú vô thượng, thần chú sánh với điều vô song, thần chú diệt trừ mọi khổ đau-là chân thật vì không hư vọng. Thần chú của Bát-nhã Ba-la-mật được tuyên thuyết như sau:

Tadyatha gate gate paragate parasamgate bodhi svaha!

Này Shariputra, các vị Bồ-tát-những bậc đại nhân-nên tu tập Bát-nhã Ba-la-mật theo cách này."

Cho đến đoạn này, Bồ-tát Quán Tự Tại đã trình bày giáo lý về tánh Không một cách chi tiết, chủ yếu dành cho những hành giả có trí tuệ. Giờ đây, ngài chuyển sang trình bày súc tích cho những hành giả có trí tuệ phi thường, dưới hình thức một bài thần chú. Trước tiên, ngài tán thán Bát-nhã Ba-la-mật. Kinh văn ghi:

"Vì vậy, cần biết rằng thần chú của Bát-nhã Ba-la-mật-thần chú của đại trí tuệ... vì nó không hư vọng."

Bát Nhã Ba-la-mật được gọi là "thần chú" vì năng lực đưa hành giả vượt qua đại dương sinh tử luân hồi (samsara). Cách gọi này cũng tương ứng với nghĩa gốc của từ "mantra" - tức là "bảo vệ tâm". Trí tuệ chứng ngộ tánh Không có khả năng bảo hộ hành giả khỏi vô minh chấp ngã. Thần chú này được gọi là "đại trí thần chú" vì có thể đoạn trừ mọi loại vô minh và các phiền não phát sinh từ đó. Đồng thời, nó còn được tôn xưng là "vô thượng thần chú", bởi không có con đường nào vượt trội hơn trí tuệ ba-la-mật trong việc dẫn đến quả vị giác ngộ.

Thần chú này được gọi là "thần chú sánh ngang với điều vô song" vì trí tuệ Ba-la-mật giúp hành giả thành tựu quả vị bình đẳng với quả vị Phật-quả vị không gì sánh được. Trí tuệ ba-la-mật như một phương dược tối thắng có thể diệt trừ mọi khổ đau và nhân của khổ đau, do đó được tôn xưng là "thần chú diệt trừ mọi khổ đau". Trí tuệ ba-la-mật thấy rõ chân như của các pháp, nơi đó không có sai biệt giữa hiện tướng và thực tại. Vì vậy, nó là chân thật, không hư vọng.

Thần chú được tuyên thuyết là:

TADYATHA GATE GATE PARAGATE PARASAMGATE BODHI SVAHA

Thông thường, các Kinh thuộc hệ Bát-nhã Ba-la-mật đều có một chủ đề hiển lộ là **tánh Không**, và một chủ đề ẩn là **các giai đoạn của đạo lộ liên hệ đến trí tuệ chứng ngộ tánh Không.** Thần chú trên chính là sự thể hiện chủ đề ẩn của Bát-nhã Tâm Kinh, và được tuyên thuyết bằng tiếng Phạn:

- **Tadyatha** – "Như vậy đó"
- **Gate Gate** – "Hãy đi, hãy đi"
- **Paragate** – "Hãy đi vượt khỏi"
- **Parasamgate** – "Hãy đi vượt qua hoàn toàn"
- **Bodhi Svaha** – "An trụ trong nền tảng của Giác ngộ"

Khi gộp lại, thần chú có nghĩa là:

"Hãy đi, hãy đi, hãy đi vượt khỏi, hãy đi vượt qua hoàn toàn, an trụ trong nền tảng của Giác ngộ."

Thoạt nghe, có thể câu này vẫn chưa rõ ràng. Tuy nhiên, nếu đặt nó trong mối liên hệ với năm đạo lộ, ý nghĩa sẽ sáng tỏ hơn. Bồ-tát Quán

Tự Tại khuyến khích hành giả bước vào năm đạo lộ như sau: Hai chữ "Hãy đi" đầu tiên tương ứng với đạo tích lũy và đạo chuẩn bị. "Hãy đi vượt khỏi" và "Hãy đi vượt qua hoàn toàn" lần lượt tương ứng với đạo kiến và đạo tu.

Cuối cùng, "Bodhi Svaha" là lời khuyến khích bước vào đạo vô học - tức là trạng thái Giác ngộ viên mãn, không còn gì phải tu học thêm. Câu thần chú này phác họa các giai đoạn của đạo lộ mà hành giả cần tuần tự tiến tu để đạt đến Phật quả, tức là sự giải thoát hoàn toàn. Bồ-tát Quán Tự Tại xác quyết với Xá-lợi-phất rằng: đây chính là cách thực hành trí tuệ ba-la-mật thâm sâu, như lời trong kinh văn:

"Này Xá-lợi-phất, các vị Bồ-tát, những bậc Đại nhân, nên tu tập trí tuệ ba-la-mật theo cách này."

Đây là phần kết của lời đáp mà Bồ-tát Quán Tự Tại đưa ra trước câu hỏi của Xá-lợi-phất.

KẾT LUẬN

Lời xác chứng và biểu lộ hoan hỷ

Kinh văn ghi:

"Ngay khi ấy, Đức Thế Tôn xuất khỏi tam-muội và tán thán Thánh Bồ-tát Quán Tự Tại, bậc Đại sĩ: 'Hay lắm! Hay lắm! Hay lắm! Này thiện nam tử, quả thật đúng như vậy, chính nên như vậy! Phải hành trì Bát-nhã Ba-la-mật thâm sâu đúng như lời ngươi đã tuyên thuyết. Vì nếu thực hành như thế, ngay cả chư Như Lai cũng sẽ khởi tâm hoan hỷ.'"

Cho đến đoạn này, trong suốt cuộc đối thoại giữa Xá Lợi Phất và Bồ-tát Quán Tự Tại, Đức Phật đang an trụ trong thiền định. Vào lúc này, Đức Phật xuất khỏi thiền định, tán thán và xác chứng phần trình bày về trí tuệ ba-la-mật thâm sâu của Bồ-tát Quán Tự Tại qua lời: "Hay lắm! Hay lắm! Này thiện nam tử, quả thật đúng như vậy, chính nên như vậy! Phải hành trì Bát-nhã Ba-la-mật thâm sâu đúng như ngươi đã tuyên thuyết. Khi ấy, chư Như Lai cũng sẽ hoan hỷ." Đoạn này trong Bát-nhã Tâm Kinh thuộc giáo pháp do chính Đức Phật tuyên thuyết.

Phần kết của Tâm Kinh nói về việc hội chúng bày tỏ sự hoan hỷ. Kinh văn ghi: "Khi Đức Thế Tôn tuyên thuyết những lời này, Tôn giả Xá Lợi Phất, Bồ-tát Quán Tự Tại, bậc Đại sĩ, cùng toàn thể đại chúng—bao gồm chư thiên, nhân loại, a-tu-la, và càn-thát-bà—đều hoan hỷ, tán thán lời Đức Thế Tôn đã dạy."

Sau đó, Đức Phật tán thán Bồ-tát Quán Tự Tại, và tất cả những ai hiện diện trong hội chúng—bao gồm chư thiên, loài người, a-tu-la và càn-thát-bà—đều hoan hỷ, tán thán Đức Phật đã tuyên thuyết giáo pháp quý báu này.

Lời kết và Hồi hướng

Tâm Kinh thật thâm sâu, và chúng ta đã quán chiếu nhiều lợi lạc từ bản kinh này. Giờ đây, cần đem sự hiểu biết ấy vào thực hành—một trong những phương cách là qua thiền quán phân tích.

Đối với những ai hành trì tâm linh hằng ngày, trước khi bắt đầu thời khóa, hãy dành vài phút để thiền quán đơn giản dựa trên lối phân tích được rút ra từ những bài kệ do Bồ-tát Long Thọ trước tác sau đây:

"Con người không phải là đất, không phải là nước,
Không phải là lửa, không phải là gió, không phải là hư không,
Không phải là thức, cũng không phải là tất cả những thứ ấy.
Vậy có con người nào tồn tại ngoài những thứ đó chăng?"

Cũng như con người không thật có,
Vì chỉ là sự kết hợp của sáu yếu tố,
Thì mỗi yếu tố ấy
Cũng không thật có vì vốn do hợp thành."

Những bài kệ này hướng dẫn ta thiền quán về tánh Không của ngã và các pháp. Hãy bắt đầu bằng cách khởi lên một cảm giác "tôi" thật mãnh liệt. Bạn có thể sử dụng bất kỳ phương pháp nào giúp làm khởi hiện cảm giác ấy—chẳng hạn như hồi tưởng một sự việc khiến bạn phẫn nộ, như bị người khác xúc phạm.

Khi cảm giác ngã sống động này khởi lên, hãy quán sát xem nó hiện khởi như thế nào. Thông thường, cái "tôi" ấy có vẻ rất kiên cố, độc lập—tựa như nó tồn tại một cách riêng biệt, không nương tựa vào bất kỳ điều gì khác. Nếu nó xuất hiện như thế thực sự hiện hữu, thì ta cần tiếp tục khảo sát sâu hơn.

Ta tự hỏi: "Cái tôi này ở đâu?" Ta phải truy tìm cái 'tôi' có vẻ như rất kiên cố ấy. Lý do là: nếu một điều gì đó thực sự tồn tại một cách tự tính, thì hẳn ta phải có thể tìm thấy nó—chỉ ra nó và nói: "Đây rồi, nó ở đây!"

Vậy hãy quay lại bài kệ của Long Thọ: "Người không phải đất, không phải nước..." Trước tiên, hãy quan sát phần cứng trong thân thể—đó có phải là "tôi" không? Còn các phần chất lỏng—yếu tố nước—có phải là "tôi" không? Khi ta xét từng phần và loại trừ từng yếu tố một, ta sẽ đi đến kết luận rằng: không có gì—thậm chí đến một nguyên tử nhỏ nhất—là "tôi". Kế đến, ta khảo sát tâm, thức—có phần nào là bản ngã chăng? Bàn tay có phải là "tôi"? Cái đầu có phải là "tôi"? Không.

Qua tiến trình loại trừ này, ta có thể đạt đến một sự nhận ra: "Ồ, không hề có cái 'tôi' nào thật sự hiện hữu." Trong một buổi giảng trực tuyến gần đây, Thánh Đức chia sẻ rằng khi Ngài có được sự chứng ngộ ấy, một cảm giác sợ hãi liền khởi lên: "Ồ, không có cái 'tôi' nào cả!" Nhưng Ngài nói rằng nỗi sợ ấy là một dấu hiệu tốt—nó phản ánh một phần kinh nghiệm trực tiếp về tánh Không. Khi đạt đến kết luận đó, hãy để tâm an trú trong khoảng không sinh khởi từ sự phủ định cái "tôi" vốn được chấp là có tự tính. Hãy cố gắng an trú trong trạng thái nhận biết tánh Không ấy càng lâu càng tốt.

Tuy nhiên, điều hết sức quan trọng cần hiểu là: dù ta phủ nhận một cái "tôi" tồn tại một cách chân thật, ta không hề phủ nhận sự hiện hữu của "tôi" hay "ngã." Chúng ta không nói rằng hoàn toàn không có cái ngã nào cả. Điều được nhận ra ở đây là: cái ngã không hiện hữu một cách kiên cố, độc lập như ta vẫn thường cảm nhận. Thay vào đó, cái "tôi" tồn tại một cách phụ thuộc vào nền tảng của nó—chính là năm uẩn. Cái "tôi" là một danh xưng do tâm quy ước mà gán lên tập hợp của các uẩn ấy.

Điều này có thể khiến ta lầm tưởng rằng tuy cái "tôi" không có tự tính, nhưng nền tảng của nó—các uẩn—lại tồn tại một cách tự tính. Để phá trừ quan niệm sai lầm đó, ta hãy quán chiếu bài kệ thứ hai sau đây:

> "Cũng như cái người không thật có,
> Vì chỉ là sự tập hợp của sáu thành tố,
> Thì từng thành tố ấy
> Cũng không thật có, vì đều là hợp thành."

Cũng như cái ngã không thật có hay không tồn tại một cách tự tính vì chỉ là một tập hợp (sự kết hợp của các thành phần và sự gán đặt nhãn hiệu), thì mỗi thành tố trong sáu thành tố ấy cũng không tồn tại tự tính. Thông qua sự quán chiếu này, ta nhận ra rằng ngay cả các uẩn—sắc, thọ, tưởng, hành, thức v.v.—cũng đều rỗng không tự tính.

Một lần nữa, hãy cố gắng duy trì trạng thái tỉnh thức về tánh Không càng lâu càng tốt. Cuối cùng, ta sẽ đạt đến nhận thức rằng mọi pháp, kể cả cái ngã, đều do duyên khởi. Cái "tôi" chỉ là một danh xưng được gán đặt lên một tập hợp các phần—giống như "chiếc xe" là tên gọi mà ta gán cho sự sắp xếp của bánh xe, trục xe và các bộ phận khác. Vì vậy, con người không hiện hữu một cách tự tính, và các phần hợp thành cũng vậy. Cái ngã tồn tại tùy thuộc vào các nhân, duyên, thành phần cấu tạo và sự gán danh.

Những gì tôi chia sẻ ở đây chỉ là phần nổi của tảng băng trôi. Đây là phần dẫn nhập vào Tâm Kinh. Bản văn thâm sâu này có thể được nghiên cứu và truyền dạy ở nhiều cấp độ khác nhau. Những điều tôi trình bày chỉ là bước khởi đầu. Vì vậy, đừng dừng lại tại đây. Hãy tiếp tục học hỏi và quán chiếu sâu xa hơn về chủ đề này.

Luôn ghi nhớ tánh Không. Hãy duy trì sự tỉnh thức ấy trong mọi hành xử của bạn. Điều này đặc biệt hữu ích trong các tương tác hằng ngày. Mọi phân biệt và phiền não của chúng ta đều khởi sinh từ sự chấp thủ sai lầm—niềm tin sai lầm rằng các pháp tồn tại một cách kiên cố, có tự tính. Ta nhìn kẻ thù và những vấn đề như thể chúng hiện hữu tự thân.Chúng ta nhìn mọi pháp như những thực thể cố định và thật có, chứ không phải là những kiến tạo của tâm thức. Nhưng nếu ta có thể nhận ra rằng các pháp chỉ là những danh xưng do tâm gán đặt, chỉ là sự quy ước áp lên một nền tảng, thì sự chấp thủ nơi ta sẽ dần dần được nới lỏng. Cái nắm giữ chặt chẽ ấy sẽ bắt đầu được buông xả. Và từ đó, sự an tĩnh sẽ từ từ khởi sinh trong nội tâm. Nguyện cầu mọi điều tốt lành đến với bạn.

Nhờ công đức này, nguyện cho tất cả chúng sinh
Viên mãn hai sự tích lũy: phước đức và trí tuệ,
Và chứng đắc hai thân thánh
Phát sinh từ công đức của phước đức và trí tuệ.

VỀ TÁC GIẢ

Drupa Rinpoche (Lobsang Yeshi) là một vị Tăng sĩ Phật giáo Tây Tạng và là vị thứ 7 trong dòng truyền thừa Drupa Rinpoche. Ngài sinh ra tại Ấn Độ và vào năm 1988, được Đức Đạt Lai Lạt Ma thứ 14 chính thức công nhận là hóa thân của Drupa Rinpoche đời thứ 6, Shedrup Tenpai Gyaltsen. Ngài hiện là viện trưởng của Tu viện Drupa tại vùng Kham, miền Đông Tây Tạng.

Drupa Rinpoche (Lobsang Yeshi) là một vị Tăng sĩ Phật giáo Tây Tạng và là vị thứ bảy trong dòng truyền thừa Drupa Rinpoche. Ngài sinh tại Ấn Độ và vào năm 1988, được Đức Đạt Lai Lạt Ma đời thứ mười bốn xác nhận là hóa thân của Drupa Rinpoche đời thứ sáu, Shedrup Tenpai Gyaltsen. Ngài hiện là viện trưởng Tu viện Drupa tại vùng Kham, miền Đông Tây Tạng.

Rinpoche có học vị *Geshe* (tiến sĩ Phật học truyền thống) từ Tu viện Drepung Loselling (Nam Ấn Độ), bằng Cử nhân Tâm lý học tại Đại học HELP (Malaysia), và bằng Thạc sĩ Khoa học chuyên ngành Tâm lý học Tích cực từ Đại học Life (Georgia, Hoa Kỳ). Hiện nay, Ngài là giáo thọ thường trú tại Trung tâm Phật pháp Kachoeling ở Minneapolis, đồng thời là người sáng lập tổ chức phi lợi nhuận mang tên **Drupa Monastery – Oasis of Dharma** tại Saint Paul, Minnesota. Trước đây, Ngài từng là nhà nghiên cứu tại Trường Y tế Công cộng, Đại học Minnesota, và hiện đang là Tăng sĩ tình nguyện (Chaplain Phật giáo) tại Trung tâm Y tế Hạt Hennepin.

KINH VĂN GỐC

Bát-nhã Tâm Kinh

(*Kinh Tâm của Trí Tuệ Ba-la-mật Siêu Việt*)

Đảnh lễ Đức Bà Bhagavatī Prajñāpāramitā!

Như vầy tôi đã nghe. Một thời, Đức Thế Tôn ngự tại núi Linh Thứu, thành Vương Xá (Rājgṛha), cùng với đại chúng Tỳ-kheo và đại chúng Bồ-tát.

Bấy giờ, Đức Thế Tôn nhập vào tam-muội về các pháp được gọi là "Quán chiếu sâu xa." Đồng thời, Bồ-tát Quán Tự Tại, bậc Đại sĩ, đang quán chiếu hành trì trí tuệ ba-la-mật thâm sâu, thấy rằng năm uẩn đều không có tự tánh.

Khi ấy, nhờ oai lực của Phật, Tôn giả Xá Lợi Phất bạch Bồ-tát Quán Tự Tại, bậc Đại sĩ, rằng: "Thưa Bồ-tát, thiện nam tử nào muốn tu hành Bát-nhã Ba-la-mật thâm sâu thì nên học hành như thế nào?"

Khi ấy, Bồ-tát Quán Tự Tại, bậc Đại sĩ, đáp lại Tôn giả Xá Lợi Phất như sau: "Này Xá Lợi Phất, thiện nam tử hay thiện nữ nhân nào muốn hành trì Bát-nhã Ba-la-mật thâm sâu nên quán chiếu như thế này: nên thấy năm uẩn đều không có tự tánh. Sắc tức là Không, Không tức là sắc. Sắc chẳng khác Không, Không chẳng khác sắc. Thọ, tưởng, hành, thức cũng đều như vậy."

Vì vậy, này Xá Lợi Phất, tất cả các pháp đều là tánh Không; không có tướng riêng; không sinh, không diệt; không nhơ, không tịnh; không thiếu, không đủ. Do đó, này Xá Lợi Phất, trong tánh Không: không có sắc, không có thọ, không có tưởng, không có hành, không có thức; không có mắt, không có tai, không có mũi, không có lưỡi, không có thân, không có ý; không có sắc, thanh, hương, vị, xúc, pháp; không có nhãn giới, nhĩ giới, tỷ giới, thiệt giới, thân giới, ý giới; không có nhãn thức giới, nhĩ thức giới, tỷ thức giới, thiệt thức giới, thân thức giới, ý thức giới; không có vô minh, cũng không có sự diệt tận của vô minh; cho đến không có già chết, cũng không có sự diệt tận của già chết.

Tương tự, không có khổ, tập, diệt, đạo; không có trí tuệ, không có chứng đắc, cũng không có không chứng đắc. Vì vậy, này Xá Lợi Phất, do các vị Bồ Tát không có sở đắc, nên nương tựa nơi Bát-nhã Ba-la-mật và an trụ trong đó. Vì tâm không bị chướng ngại nên không có sợ hãi; vượt qua hoàn toàn mọi điên đảo vọng tưởng, các ngài chứng đạt Niết-bàn rốt ráo. Tất cả chư Phật trong ba đời đều nương vào Bát-nhã Ba-la-mật thâm sâu mà chứng đắc Vô thượng Chánh đẳng Chánh giác.

Do đó, chân ngôn của Bát-nhã Ba-la-mật—chân ngôn của đại trí tuệ, chân ngôn vô thượng, chân ngôn sánh bằng điều vô song, chân ngôn diệt trừ mọi khổ đau—là chân thật vì không hư vọng. Chân ngôn của Bát-nhã Ba-la-mật được tuyên thuyết như sau:
[oṃ] gate gate pāragate pārasaṃgate bodhi svāhā.

"Này Xá Lợi Phất, một vị Bồ Tát, bậc đại sĩ, nên tu tập Bát-nhã Ba-la-mật thâm sâu theo cách này."

Khi ấy, Đức Thế Tôn xuất khỏi tam-muội và tán thán Bồ Tát Quán Tự Tại, bậc đại sĩ, rằng: "Hay lắm, hay lắm, thiện nam tử! Quả thật là như vậy, đúng là như vậy. Nên hành trì Bát-nhã Ba-la-mật thâm sâu đúng như ngươi đã tuyên thuyết. Khi thực hành như thế, ngay cả chư Như Lai cũng sẽ hoan hỷ."

Khi Đức Thế Tôn nói lời này xong, Tôn giả Xá Lợi Phất, Bồ Tát Quán Tự Tại, bậc đại sĩ, cùng với toàn thể đại chúng và các cõi trời, người, a-tu-la, càn-thát-bà, đều hoan hỷ và tán thán lời tuyên thuyết của Đức Thế Tôn.

www.ingramcontent.com/pod-product-compliance
Lightning Source LLC
LaVergne TN
LVHW082039051026
849532LV00011B/3415